How to
Run Your Business
So You Can
Leave It in Style

How to
Run Your Business
So You Can
Leave It in Style

John H. Brown

with Irv Sternberg

American Management Association

This publication is designed to provide accurate and authoritative information in regard to the subject matter covered. It is sold with the understanding that the publisher is not engaged in rendering legal, accounting, or other professional service. If legal advice or other expert assistance is required, the services of a competent professional person should be sought.

Library of Congress Cataloging-in-Publication Data

Brown, John H., 1947–
    How to run your business so you can leave it in style / John H.
Brown with Irv Sternberg.
        p.   cm.
    ISBN 0-8144-5980-3
        1. Business enterprises—United States. 2. Estate planning—
United States. 3. Business enterprises, Sale of—United States.
4. Business enterprises—Taxation—United States. 5. Inheritance
and transfer tax—Law and legislation—United States.
I. Sternberg, Irv. II. Title.
KF1355.B76   1990
346.73'065—dc20   89-81022
[347.30665]   CIP

Printing number

10   9   8   7   6   5   4   3   2   1

To my first **employers**
from whom I learned so much
—my **parents,**
Harold and **Helen Brown**

Contents

Preface

As a business lawyer for the last fifteen years, I've seen too many good businessmen and women fall short in achieving business ownership objectives. Often it was because they confused ownership objectives with business objectives such as good management, high profitability, quality products, and good service. Too often owners do not realize that these business objectives are different from—and in addition to—the objectives they should have as owners.

Hundreds of books have been written about proper management: how to make your business more profitable and how to increase the quality of your product or the level of service to your customers. It's difficult to concentrate even on these objectives because routine crises constantly interrupt your daily schedule and divert your attention. But even if you master these business objectives, simply attaining them is not enough.

I've represented hundreds of successful businesses over the years. Many were well-run, capably managed, highly profitable, and respected by their competitors and customers alike. From this experience I've learned that all business owners—someday—must leave their businesses. They must do so because they become disabled, or suffer "burnout," or desire to move on to greener pastures, or—because of the ultimate reason—they die.

When my business-owner clients started coming to me with plans to leave their businesses, I tried to help them sell out for as much as possible. Too often there was no one to sell the business to; we were forced to conclude that the only thing we could do was to shut the doors. Many times we could not even do that because the owner needed the ongoing income stream from the business to support his or her life-style.

After this happened a few times, the light bulb went on. I finally became aware that business owners must do more than simply run their businesses and also that I needed to do more than simply offer traditional legal advice to my business clients.

Since then, I've concentrated on encouraging my clients to think about the day when they will leave their businesses— for whatever reason. When that day arrives, they will want to leave on their own terms and conditions. In order to do that, preparation and planning are necessary.

First, all owners must distinguish between their business needs and their needs as owners. That is the central idea of this book.

I've divided the book into three parts. Each part discusses an essential element in your planning as a business owner:

1. How to make the business enterprise valuable.
2. How to find a way of converting that value into cash for your eventual use.
3. How to integrate your personal needs, income, financial planning, and estate planning with the workings of your business.

To create value, you must go beyond the basic needs of making money and expanding and managing your business on a day-to-day basis. You must set aside time to plan and become knowledgeable in three specific areas: (1) minimizing corporate and personal income taxes, (2) retaining and motivating key employees, and (3) practicing "preventive maintenance" to avoid problems which can threaten the value of your business.

Chapters 1 through 4 suggest a new way to look at "success in business" and introduce you to the idea of planning for your future with the help of a carefully selected team of professional advisors. This part also shows you how to use your lawyer effectively, offers advice on motivating your key

employees, and provides you with an overview of tax fundamentals.

To convert value into cash, you must transfer your ownership and control. In other words, you must leave your
business. When that day arrives, you will want to leave with
the biggest pile of cash you can collect. This can be accomplished only if you plan ahead. Too often, a change in ownership and control is ignored until some unforeseen event occurs, such as disability or the death of an owner, a family
crisis, or a mid-life change in life-style. Or the owner is simply
burned out.

Chapters 5 through 9 discuss the various ways you may
leave your business and show how to select—and plan for—
the method that's best for you. Chapter 9 explains why you
need a business continuity agreement—the most important
document in your business.

To integrate your personal goals with your business goals,
you must think of your business as an investment asset, like
shares of IBM stock or that limited partnership you bought
into. If you're like most business owners, your business represents the bulk of your assets. You must be able to draw funds
from this asset to provide for your retirement and to create an
estate for your family in the event of your death.

Chapters 10 and 11 describe how to do the kind of
financial and estate planning that will minimize Uncle Sam's
share of your hard-earned money so that you can retire comfortably with the knowledge that your family also will be
provided for. Chapter 12 summarizes the ten-step planning
you must do to achieve your *objectives as an owner,* the kind
of planning owners seldom do.

Why don't business owners plan for themselves? Caught
up in the demands of starting and operating their businesses,
most owners are too preoccupied with handling daily, sometimes hourly, crises to think about their futures. They're too
busy fighting alligators to even think about draining the
swamp!

My intention is to make you aware of the need to use your
business to plan for your future. I'll show you step-by-step

how to identify and achieve your personal, long-term objectives. You'll not only be able to wrestle the alligators into submission, but you also may turn that swamp into fertile farmland, sell it to a developer for top dollar, and retire to live happily ever after wearing alligator boots!

I rely heavily on case studies taken from the files of my law firm. The situations I describe actually occurred, although in every case I've changed the names of the individuals, and sometimes the circumstances, to protect their identities. I employ these case histories because they help demonstrate my points in human terms. The story of Helen Birkel does such a good job of illustrating these points that I'll tell you about her right now.

Helen is the best businesswoman I've ever represented. Starting in the early 1960s with a small retail jewelry store, she expanded her business steadily, adding many locations until her firm became a regional leader noted for jewelry she designed herself. Fortunately, she realized that the business was growing beyond her capacity to manage it, and the day was fast-approaching when she would have to slow down or even sell out.

Several of her brothers and sisters had been active in the business, but none had the desire, willingness, or ability to buy out the entire chain of stores; nor were there any key employees who could be considered a market for her interests. Realizing this, she took an important step: She hired a business consultant to help prepare her and the business for its eventual sale. Under the consultant's direction, she also retained a new accountant and a new lawyer—me.

Helen's new advisory team implemented an employee stock option plan (ESOP) and sold part of her stock to the plan in order to obtain favorable tax treatment and provide additional motivation to her employees after her departure. The consultant then instituted an executive search and found a bright, aggressive young man to be president who was attracted not only by the challenge, but also by the incentive package which included an enticing deferred compensation program—with "golden handcuff" provisions. These provisions bound the new president to Helen's company by requiring that he remain employed for five years before becoming entitled to the deferred compensation.

With a solidified executive staff and motivated work force, Helen was able to sell the rest of her stock to a third party, a competitor she had known for years, at a substantial profit. The terms of the sale provided that she remain with the business, doing what she'd always enjoyed: designing fine jewelry. The last time I heard from her, she was still at it. She was not working for the money—she had all she needed—but for the fun of it. In fact, she installed a vigorous gifting program for her children and grandchildren in order to minimize her estate tax liability.

Helen has achieved what should be every business owner's objective. She started and operated a profitable business, then converted that success into hard cash. This enabled her to achieve her personal financial and estate planning goals. By having the foresight to gather around her a competent group of advisors, and by committing herself to the planning process, Helen accomplished all her objectives—and made the rest of us envious.

Unlike Helen Birkel, too many business owners would rather *act* than *contemplate*. "Ready, fire, aim" is truly their *modus operandi*. Often my job is to be sure they aim at carefully selected targets before they fire. Aiming, or planning first, is what this book is about.

Acknowledgments

Writing this book would have been impossible without the constant support of my employer, Minor & Brown, P.C., or the creative talents of my friend and "ghost writer," Irv Sternberg.

Minor & Brown provided me the book's raw material in the form of its clients and the methods and procedures developed over the years in order to properly plan for those clients. Just as importantly, my law firm supplied much needed assistance in the writing and rewriting of this book. Two lawyers, Barbara Wells and James Thomas, carefully reviewed the book for technical accuracy and readability. It is not unfair to observe that they took particular delight in making innumerable corrections to their boss's book. Although I am confident that their many months of merriment contributed greatly to the accuracy and effectiveness of the book, they are not responsible for the end result. Nor are Irv's fellow writers, Franklin "Bill" Muth and Charles Riccio, Jr., who also contributed helpful ideas. Custom (and Irv) dictate that I bear that burden alone.

I also wish to acknowledge two other members of Minor & Brown, P.C. First, I thank my invaluable assistant, Jeanie Tae, who typed much of the early manuscript, and second, Kathy Carroll, who as the law office administrator took charge of the administrative details surrounding the writing and publishing of the book.

Finally, and perhaps most unreservedly, I thank my fellow shareholders at the law firm: Ned Minor and Paul Rumler. Their unwavering perseverance is remarkable not only for its duration but also because it must be motivated by some quality more noble than financial reward—of which there is but little hope.

Irv tells me it is inappropriate to acknowledge his efforts and contributions to this book since I have already done so on the cover. However, for once I will ignore his advice. I thank him for the countless hours he spent organizing my material, editing and rewriting chapters as first drafts were completed, reediting subsequent drafts, forcing me to maintain a writing schedule and, through the use of personal example, showing me how to write well.

Part I

Creating and Preserving Value Within the Business

Creating and preserving value is the first of three goals that you, as the business owner, must pursue if you are to achieve your ultimate goal of leaving your business in style. Chapters 1 through 4 help start you toward that goal.

First, I ask you to consider a new definition of "success" and accept the challenge of learning certain "owner skills" with the help of a solid team of advisors. Next, I show you how to avoid unnecessary litigation by practicing "preventive maintenance" through the use of a legal audit and other methods. And I introduce you to the year-end review—the most effective way to use your advisory team.

A critical element in creating and preserving value in your business is knowing how to motivate and keep your key employees. All of Chapter 3 is devoted to this topic. Finally, I end this section by discussing the tax fundamentals that affect your business. This discussion won't make you a tax expert, but it will give you the insights you need to employ your advisors effectively.

1

When You're Too Busy Fighting Alligators

Redefining "success in business" and planning to achieve what you want and need

You own a profitable and growing business that provides a lot of what you desire: income, wealth, an identity, challenge, stimulation, satisfaction, and pride. By all conventional yardsticks, you are a *success*. Well done!

But wait a minute. Despite these positive signs, your business may be failing you in another way. It depends on how you define *success*. I propose a new definition—one that says success in business is measured not by how well the business operates under your ownership and not by the benefits it provides, but by the rewards it will bestow when you leave it. Because in the end, what you really want and need from your business is the ability to leave it—and eventually you will—*under the most favorable conditions*.

There is only one way you as an owner can achieve that ability: You must create a plan as early as possible and stick to that plan as long as you maintain your business.

But you *do* plan, you say. True. You plan your day-to-day operations. You create production or service schedules, devise

3

...ng strategies, plot sales efforts, compile projections, generate organization plans. But this is traditional business planning; it is not the kind of planning that *business owners must do for themselves.*

What is the difference? Let's look at a case history.

A Tale of Two Partners

Shortly before I started writing this book I met with the two major owners of a thriving construction company in Denver. Despite the downturn in the local economy, this firm had been able to maintain profits and income because of the wide experience and extraordinary personal efforts of the owners.

When we set up our meeting, I assumed we would be discussing typical fiscal year-end matters—subjects like income taxes, business continuity, and estate planning. However, when we met, the owners' first words were, "Can you review this auction agreement? We're going to sell all our equipment and get out of the business."

I was shocked.

The owners, both in their early forties, explained that their efforts to maintain the business had drained them. For years they had complied with government regulations and braced for and adjusted to the changing tax code that dramatically affected the tax benefits of their multimillion-dollar investment in construction equipment. Now they no longer had the patience, desire, or stamina to continue; they convinced me they were serious about giving up their business. So we began to explore alternative ways of getting money for the company, other than through an auction of the equipment.

First we considered a sale to a third party, but the business was too large to be bought by any company other than the larger national construction firms. Feelers to those companies revealed little desire to acquire a construction company in the depressed Rocky Mountain region.

We discussed the possibility of transferring ownership by selling the firm to the employees or offering a buyout to key managers. Both ideas were rejected because, although there were important employees, none had ever been groomed to accept greater responsibilities in the organization. There was simply no one ready to take over and run the business, nor had anything been done to set up a fund for the owners' retirement.

The two owners had retained control of all of the key functions. Unless they continued in those roles, the business was unlikely to remain successful. Since the owners were unwilling to keep fighting the battle that had worn them down, they sadly decided to liquidate at auction prices, despite years of profitability.

This story illustrates an important point: A business can be both growing and profitable, even highly profitable for a long period of time, and yet have little worth beyond the "fire sale" value of its tangible assets—machinery, vehicles, office equipment, furniture, buildings, and inventory.

The Denver construction company was both profitable and growing, yet little value was created or preserved. And this was a $30 million annual sales company, not a mom-and-pop store.

How did these hardworking, experienced, knowledgeable, and successful partners find themselves in this predicament after years of dedicated involvement in building their company? *They never took the time to plan for and create a market for their stock.*

For years they devoted themselves to the day-to-day management of the business, personally handling hundreds of details, dealing with crises, putting out fires. The intensity the owners generated and the energy they expended in avoiding the alligators and making their company a success eventually led to their burnout—and the inevitability of liquidation. Reluctantly, they gave up their participation in the business; moreover, there was no one else available to keep it going.

The business disappeared. Dozens of employees lost their jobs. The owners settled for the cash earned through the sale of their tangible assets—an amount far less than the company's value as a going concern. All of this could have been avoided through proper planning.

The partners should have identified and pursued the three objectives essential to their success as I've defined them. Again, these objectives are:

.ᴏ create and preserve the value of the company.

2. To provide a means to exchange that value for money.
3. To integrate the personal, financial, and estate planning goals of the owner with his or her fundamental business objectives.

Planning for Yourself as an Owner

I said earlier that all businesses do some kind of planning. It may be a simple discussion or a document. Most of this, however, is done at the corporate level, not at the ownership level, and covers what I call the operations aspect of a business, such as a budget, a marketing plan, and perhaps an organization or administration plan for adding personnel as a company expands.

Operational planning can help keep expenses in line, boost revenues through marketing, and lay the groundwork for hiring the right people. This, in turn, can result in a profitable, valuable company. Usually short term in nature, these plans require review and substantial revisions at least annually.

But this is not the kind of planning I'll be discussing. There are numerous marketing, management, and accounting resources and advisors available to help the business owner achieve his or her goals in these areas. The kind of planning I'll discuss has the owner's objectives in mind. It is not *business planning* as much as it is *owner planning*—based on information, knowledge, and experiences gained from the business.

And not only will it make the business more profitable and more stable, but it will also provide a way for the business owner to create and obtain value when he or she decides to withdraw or retire.

Let's look again at the three owner objectives.

Creating and Preserving Value

Although the purpose of business is to make money, an objective generally perceived as being worthwhile and useful, most entrepreneurs are so dedicated to this purpose they have little or no time to spend on creating and preserving a value for their business. Nonetheless, they must find the time to acquire certain skills and knowledge. I cover these items in Part I because they are critical to achieving your long-term objectives as an owner.

Transferring Ownership and Control

Inevitably, every business owner will sooner or later leave the business. Yet few owners think about that event when they are building and running their business. In no other area is the need for planning so obvious and the lack of planning so common.

One approach is to transfer ownership and control to a group of key employees. If this approach seems feasible, you should act quickly to identify and prepare those employees for the day they will assume total responsibility for running the business. To obtain full benefit, you must implement your plan over a number of years.

For now, you should be aware of the need to plan for your eventual departure because either of the following scenarios is going to occur:

1. You will transfer ownership of the business during your lifetime because you've decided you want out. Without planning, you will probably have to liquidate it; with planning, you will be able to sell it to a third party, to key employees or co-owners, or to family members.
2. You will die or become totally disabled, and the business will have to be liquidated unless some type of business continuity agreement has been drawn up.

Integrating Personal Goals With Basic Business Objectives

Unlike sellers of IBM stock, you have no readily available market to sell your business to. This is a serious problem because it must be dovetailed with your personal planning. Estate planning and personal income tax planning, reviewed annually, are critically important (see Chapters 10 and 11).

You may at this point be asking yourself, "If these concerns are so important, why not simply have my key employees formulate solutions?" After all, if you can delegate important operational responsibilities to key employees, why not also give them the responsibility for resolving such problems? The answer lies in the nature of the objectives.

Each objective concerns the owners and their business, not the employees, no matter how dedicated. True, valued employees want your business to succeed. After all, they do have a stake—their jobs. Such employees are good managers, good operators, and good administrators. But these attributes have nothing to do with the special relationship between owners and their business. In other words, employees don't care about the owner's objectives because *ownership objectives are different from the business's objectives.*

Why should your most valued employees concern themselves with how much the business is worth, how to reduce your income taxes, how much money you want to accumulate so you can retire at age 55, or how to dispose of the business when you want to get out? These are issues that concern you, the owner, not your administrators, managers, supervisors, or hourly employees. Planning for these goals is a function that only you, the owner, can and should perform. But you don't need to do it alone; you can obtain help.

Assembling Your Advisory Team

Where do you look for this help? You turn to your advisors. Because your team of advisors is such an essential element in your business (see Chapters 2 and 10), let's review that concept now—the who, what, why, where, and how of it.

Let's start with the *why.*

Unless you've spent half your lifetime earning professional degrees, it's not likely you possess *all* the knowledge needed to achieve the objectives I've identified. Your astuteness and energy notwithstanding, you still require the services of experts whose education, training, and experience will supplement your own background and expand your knowledge. Since your decisions will be based on information, the more quality information you obtain the better your decisions will be.

Whom should you ask to join your team?

The typical entrepreneur needs the help of an accountant (preferably a CPA), a lawyer, a financial planner or insurance specialist, and, periodically, a special business consultant. All should have extensive experience in dealing with closely held businesses as opposed to being generalists in their respective fields.

What will they do for you?

Unlike your employees, these advisors will represent *you*. With your active input, they can help you gain ownership perspective, identify your ownership objectives, and show you how to go about achieving those objectives through ownership planning. As specialists, they possess a pool of knowledge and experience you can tap into to plan and run your business. And as impartial observers of your business, they can provide the objectivity you need in a variety of situations.

Remember, you don't have to give these advisors all of your work immediately. Start them out slowly and see how they perform. For example, you might ask a CPA to handle your personal tax return before you turn over your other accounts and tax work; you could limit a new attorney to estate planning at the start; or you may ask your financial advisor to create a plan, but implement it yourself. These restraints may be lifted after the trial period during which you assess their work.

Where do you find your advisors?

All reputable professionals are members in good standing in their professional organizations. You can obtain the names of lawyers and accountants from their respective associations and societies in your state. The membership of The Institute of Certified Financial Planners in Denver and the International

Association for Financial Planning in Atlanta comprise the majority of practicing financial planners. Ask your business colleagues to suggest names. Their referrals can be the best, because your colleagues may have developed long-term relationships with other professionals. Just be certain those professionals are performing the type of planning work we're talking about here. Interview several in each discipline before making your selection.

How do you make this team work?

Once you've identified the team members, bring them together for a team meeting. Let them get to know each other. Observe them as they interact; it's important that the chemistry be good. What you're looking for are team players who listen to you and to each other so that they will translate your wishes into action.

The specific roles of each member of your advisory team—and how each will contribute to your business and your objectives as an owner—are discussed throughout.

What If You Don't Implement a Planning Strategy?

The penalty for failure of owners to implement ownership planning has been described in the example of the construction company partners. They, at least, had substantial assets they could sell, realizing a significant cash return. Not all small-business owners are so fortunate. Take the case of Dr. Orville Peterson.

Dr. Peterson was the founding partner of a group practice in orthopedic surgery. He and his three younger partners held equal interests in the practice.

I first met Dr. Peterson when he was fifty-nine years old. He had always enjoyed a pleasant life-style, and, although he struggled to put his three children through college and graduate school, he managed to get by. When we met, he told me he was tired of practicing medicine on a full-time basis and wanted to slow down before retiring in a few years.

A quick review of his financial statement indicated little in the way of assets other than his home and his financial interest in the practice. Because of his age, there wasn't much that could be done in the way of funding retirement plans. We just couldn't get enough into a retirement plan for his benefit over a few short years.

We turned to his business interest. The practice, of which Dr. Peterson was an integral part, historically had grossed more than $1 million annually. Each physician took home more than $150,000 a year in income. As the founding partner, Dr. Peterson had built much of this practice, bringing in the younger partners to help him as the practice expanded. But he never executed a business continuity agreement, which could have established value and provided a means for the partners to buy his stock.

When we approached the other physicians, they absolutely refused to purchase Dr. Peterson's stock for anything more than his share of the practice's accounts receivable, a relatively modest sum. The good doctor was chagrined and surprised at their reaction. At this point he realized—belatedly—that although he had devoted years to his practice, his patients, and his family, he had forgotten to plan for his own retirement. Now he faced limited options.

That was six years ago. Today, at age 65, he continues to work full-time and plans to do so for another three to five years to achieve the financial goals he'll need to retire comfortably without asking for assistance from his children.

In counseling business owners over the years, I've concluded that there are a number of truths that pertain to all private businesses. I now offer my Six Laws for Business Owners:

1. Businesses that don't plan, fail.
2. Businesses that have operational plans *may* succeed.
3. Businesses that plan from the business owner's perspective are the most likely to succeed.
4. Ownership planning leads to smoother day-to-day operations of the business.
5. Planning minimizes risk when the unexpected happens to the owner.

6. Ownership planning eliminates the need to make desperate, involuntary, eleventh-hour decisions when the owner wants out of a business.

Summary

The importance of *ownership planning* as opposed to conventional business planning cannot be overemphasized. What is the difference? Ownership planning is concerned with three major areas:

1. Creating and preserving value of your company.
2. Providing a means to transfer ownership and control of the business in exchange for money.
3. Integrating your personal, financial, and estate planning goals with the fundamental goals of your business.

These are the themes that are developed throughout this book. My mission is to make you aware, and to persuade you, that ownership planning is inherently valuable and essential to you as a business owner.

To help you apply these themes to your own business, I've provided exercises at the end of most of the following chapters. Do them. They'll help you get the most out of this book.

2

Avoiding Lawyers and Other Roadblocks to Success

How to use your advisors to reduce your risks and preserve your business

I often feel that clients view me as the carrier of some deadly disease. Consequently, they call me only when their business life depends on it.

But just as physicians have learned to control smallpox with measured doses of vaccine, owners of closely held businesses should seek out lawyers to use in controlled amounts to avoid the scourge of litigation that could otherwise destroy a healthy company.

The litigation pox is pervasive and well documented. Many believe that a lack of moral values is the root cause for our litigious society. Former Supreme Court Justice Warren Burger once observed that people seem to want to be compensated for everything that went wrong in their lives. "Is it any wonder . . . that business for lawyers is so good?" he asked.

Another cause of the litigation proliferation must be ascribed to the very nature of the legal system. First, there are too many litigation lawyers. Second, the system is managed largely by lawyers who not only have an economic stake in preserving the system but have no incentive or experience to search for answers outside the system.

This obvious deficiency is widely recognized. Current efforts to lessen the adverse effects on the business world are under way. Known as tort reform, these efforts by most state legislatures seek to limit certain types of personal injury awards and reduce the amount of time plaintiffs have to start a lawsuit.

True reform, however, means more than simply putting caps on certain types of damages or shortening the time in which someone can sue. True reform means reducing the number of lawsuits that are filed and trying them quickly and efficiently before a body or panel best suited to judge the merits of the case.

I've long believed that commercial suits—litigation involving business matters—should be tried not by a jury but by some kind of "master" or group of masters who are experienced in business matters or the issues relevant to the case. In my opinion juries are simply too prone to making decisions from their hearts, rather than their minds. Too often they can be led to ignore the merits of the case.

The most recent glaring example of this is the Pennzoil v. Texaco case. The jury awarded $10.5 *billion* to the plaintiff, nearly causing the financial ruin of the defendant, a Fortune 500 company. Incidentally, $3 billion of this money was for punitive damages—it had nothing to do with the actual loss allegedly suffered by the defendant.

But abolishing juries involves more than reform; it is an institutional change. In fact, few countries other than the United States regularly allow jury trials in civil matters.

I also favor another fundamental change, one that would award attorney fees to the winning side. This would go a long way toward eliminating harassing lawsuits where businesses are, in effect, blackmailed into settling cases because the cost of litigating is greater than the demands being made by the plaintiff.

These are long-term solutions that can be achieved only through legislation in your state. It would be in your interest to encourage such legislation by working through your trade group or chamber of commerce.

However, legislative reform takes time. In the meantime, you will be wise to obtain immunization against the litigation virus: *Take the very thing that is the agent of the disease— lawyers—and inject them carefully into your business.* Like many vaccinations, this dosage of lawyers should be administered in measured, regular intervals.

The first dosage should be in the form of an initial *legal audit,* followed by annual *fiscal year-end reviews.* Interim booster shots may also be necessary from time to time to build up your business resistance in those areas where it may be most vulnerable.

Let's examine more closely just how these injections of lawyers will provide you the protection you need.

The Legal Audit

Most businesspeople are familiar with an audit performed by their accountant. The purpose of an accounting audit is to verify the accuracy of the financial information appearing on the company's financial statements.

A legal audit is similar in that the legal affairs of a business are subjected to an independent rigorous review by a trained professional who reviews the business's existing practices, procedures, and documents to determine if any potential legal problems exist.

The legal audit begins with a review of your basic corporate documents: the articles of incorporation, bylaws, minutes of shareholder meetings and board of director meetings, and the stock book showing all past stock transactions. The audit then looks at your operating documents—contracts with third parties, loan documents, leases, and a host of agreements regarding employment, trade secrecy, and the transfer of stock, to name a few.

The audit then examines ongoing practices and procedures for potential liability. These would include hiring and firing practices, insurance coverage, environmental issues, and workers compensation and unemployment compensation issues.

To continue the medical analogy, a legal audit is like a complete physical examination aimed at discovering problems while they are easily treatable. Most of us, however, are far more attentive to our body's physical signals than we are to the warning symptoms in our businesses. When the legal audit uncovers a problem, action can almost always be taken that is quick, economical, and complete. If the problem is allowed to fester until a third party—a disgruntled employee, an irate vendor, the IRS—brings it to your attention, a solution is seldom cheap and usually found only after negotiation and involvement of other parties such as lawyers, accountants, and members of your work force.

Once the problem has reached this stage, the remedy is seldom final, addressing only the immediate symptom, such as dealing with a particular employee complaint, not the underlying cause, which might be the absence of a good employee manual or the presence of a poor one. Remember, too, the nature of dealing with legal problems is to arrive at a compromise. Even in those situations where your business is completely victorious, the battle always exacts a toll—of your time, energy, attention, and money. Benjamin Franklin, the consummate businessman, said it best: "An ounce of prevention is worth a pound of cure."

The Fiscal Year-End Review

The second linchpin of the business protection program is faithful adherence to the fiscal year-end process. This step is *the single most important prevention and planning tool available to the closely held business owner.*

The concept is simple. Once a year, about forty-five days

before the business's fiscal year-end, your attorney should provide you with an agenda and send copies to your other advisors—your CPA and your financial planner. It might look like the agenda shown in Exhibit 2-1.

Along with the agenda, your attorney includes a checklist covering the items shown in Exhibit 2-2.

A meeting is then held with you and your advisors about twenty days before the fiscal year-end. This allows the ac-

Exhibit 2-1. **Fiscal year-end outline.**

I. Review of Business Income Tax Status.
   A. Initial determination of income tax liability.
   B. Existing methods of reducing income tax liability.
   C. Consideration of new methods to reduce income tax liability as appropriate.

II. Additional Corporate Considerations.
   A. Business continuity.
   B. Business expansion/contraction.
   C. Employee considerations.
   D. Business contracts and forms.
   E. Banking considerations.
   F. Miscellaneous.

III. Individual Planning Considerations.
   A. Current income tax status and methods to reduce income tax liability.
   B. Financial planning considerations.
   C. Estate planning considerations.

IV. Goal-Setting Conclusions.
   A. Business goals.
   B. Individual goals.

V. Business Opportunities.

Exhibit 2-2. Legal audit checklist.

- ☐ Appointment of officers and election of directors to serve the corporation during the next fiscal year.
- ☐ Resignations of directors and officers.
- ☐ Contributions to retirement plans.
- ☐ Grant of bonuses to shareholders/employees.
- ☐ Salary changes for shareholders/employees.
- ☐ Election or revocation of a Subchapter S election.
- ☐ Changes in the registered office or agent.
- ☐ Loans to the corporation from shareholders.
- ☐ Final repayment of loans owed by the corporation.
- ☐ Loans made by the corporation to shareholders, directors, or employees.
- ☐ Loans made by the corporation to others.
- ☐ Final repayment of loans made by the corporation.
- ☐ Changes in banks.
- ☐ Substantial capital expenditures for equipment or leasehold improvements.
- ☐ Substantial investments of capital.
- ☐ Substantial changes in business operations.
- ☐ Expected need for capital for substantial business expansion and growth.
- ☐ Adoption or amendment of any retirement plans maintained by the corporation.
- ☐ Adoption or amendment of stock buy-and-sell agreements.
- ☐ Adoption or amendment of employment agreements.
- ☐ Adoption or amendment of wage continuation plans, medical expense reimbursement plans, and Section 89 plans.
- ☐ Grant or exercise of stock options.
- ☐ Payment of death benefits.
- ☐ Payment of substantial charitable contributions.
- ☐ Adoption or amendment of deferred compensation plans.
- ☐ Purchase of life insurance plans.
- ☐ Purchase of disability income insurance plans.
- ☐ Purchase of health insurance plans.
- ☐ Execution of leases.

---

countant to review eleven months of operation and to make tentative determinations of projected income tax liability for your company and for you personally.

The purpose of the meeting is communication. You need to know your tax exposure and any income tax and legal developments that have occurred during the year that might affect your operation. Your advisors need to know not only what you have accomplished during the year, but also your future plans. Finally, each advisor must learn what the other advisors have been doing for you and what suggestions they have. This ensures coordination of your legal, tax, and financial planning objectives. The meeting also allows you to obtain input from all of your advisors on specific topics, rather than trying to reach each of them individually for their views—not an effective use of their time or your money.

In short, the fiscal year-end meeting is an important and unique way to use your advisors to elicit and exchange vital information. I can't emphasize enough the importance of this need to communicate—to plan, to prevent problems from arising, and to resolve small problems before they become insurmountable.

The Year-End Agenda

Let's review the fiscal year-end agenda in some detail.

The example included above is one my law firm developed and has refined over several years. I suggest you present a copy of this agenda to your advisors and ask them if they would be willing to meet *as a group* to engage in the fiscal year-end process. You might even suggest that they not charge you their full fee for the initial meeting, because it may be as helpful to them professionally (as a learning experience) as it is to you.

Review of Business Income Tax Status

The planning process always starts here. Advisors like to say that taxes shouldn't drive business decisions, but that sound business decisions drive themselves. In fact, a major part of the advisor's job is to minimize your tax consequences at every level.

The first item we like to see is your *projected taxable income.* We compare it to the projection made at the last fiscal year-end meeting. This gives us a quick idea of how close the business came to meeting its projections. If it fell far short of its projected taxable income, the causes must be examined as we proceed through the agenda.

When we look at *income tax liability,* we would like to project future tax liability as well as look at the past two years' tax bill. It does little good to move a potential income tax consequence to a future year if it results in a greater tax liability. Similarly, it may do a lot of good to create a large tax loss in the current year if we can carry that loss back to a previous year in which significant taxes were paid.

For an example of this, let's head out to a particular ranch I recall in southeastern Colorado.

Home on the Thibodeaux Ranch

The five members of the Thibodeaux family were all in their forties or fifties when they became interested in buying their mother's share of the family ranch—Thibodeaux Ranch, Inc. (TRI). Their father had died about a year and a half earlier, and at the time I met them, the business was a substantial operation.

Shortly before the father died—and since then—the mother had been selling off equipment and stored crops and had leased all the land to local farmers and ranchers.

Before I began serious planning, I followed my own advice and immediately involved a good CPA firm. We needed to determine the value of TRI so that we could establish a fair purchase price and plan a way for the offspring to buy the ranch from their mother with the least amount of taxes possible. In reviewing the financial information, the accountant quickly discovered that TRI had paid about $250,000 worth of taxes in each of the preceding two years.

When the elder Thibodeaux was alive, normal farm operations were usually break-even because he was able to juggle income from crop sales and cattle sales from year to year as needed to minimize taxes. Before designing the purchase of Mrs. Thibodeaux's stock, we decided to recapture the $500,000 in taxes paid in the preceding two years.

This was accomplished by creating a large tax loss for the current year as well as planning for a large tax loss the next year. Of course, it does no good to create a loss unless the loss itself is useful to the owners. In this case, because the children had been performing substantial services without pay, including selling equipment and crops, managing leases, and overseeing farm operations, we made them paid employees. It was determined that they could be paid relatively high salaries to reflect not only their ongoing services, but also their past, uncompensated contributions.

At the same time, we implemented a *defined benefit retirement plan* that, because of the relatively older ages of the children, allowed us to contribute a significant amount to the plan. The combination of high salaries and large retirement plan contributions created a $250,000 annual tax loss at the corporate level. After two years of large losses, our plan was to convert the regular corporation to an S corporation and proceed with normal farm expenditures. We believed that our plan to attack the large tax liabilities of the past was aggressive but defensible. All of the loss at the corporate level was used to directly benefit the family.

The net result was that the government each year wrote a $250,000 check to the company that was used as a large down payment for Mrs. Thibodeaux's stock! Our clients thought their advisors were brilliant, but I knew that the Thibodeaux family was lucky. Usually, the victims of nonplanning have little recourse.

One of the purposes of ongoing planning is to avoid extreme peaks or valleys in corporate taxable income. If you are able to anticipate large increases through proper tax planning, much can be done to minimize the actual tax cost. These methods include

- Shifting income taxation from one year to the next.
- Implementing tax reduction devices, such as qualified retirement plans, medical expense reimbursement plans, and the payment of large bonuses.

- Increasing deductible payments to shareholders, such as rents for equipment or buildings that may be owned individually by the business owner and leased to the business.

If these methods are already in place, see if you can increase their use to reduce tax liability. Before reducing corporate taxes, however, you must first determine how much money must *remain* at the corporate level to fuel future business growth. This is called *accumulating capital within the business*. The emphasis on minimizing taxes should not replace the clear need to ensure that the business has adequate capital to conduct its business and to grow.

As you know, growth requires capital—money—to hire additional employees, to expand the physical plant, and to conduct marketing and related services. Unfortunately, this money is almost always spent before its benefits—increased cash receipts—are realized.

Obtaining financing from banks to fuel this growth is expensive, hard to get, and potentially dangerous. Most businesses that fail do so because they lack adequate capitalization. They are overleveraged at the bank, or they simply have no capital available when the business doesn't perform as expected; they have no reserve and are unable to sustain themselves during a period of slow activity. This is as true of a major airline as it is of the corner drugstore.

The importance of the planning process, then, is to determine how much capital will be needed to fund future growth. That money generally must be kept at the corporate level. However, if personal income tax brackets are lower, the money can be paid to you as the business owner. You can then lend it back to the business or use it personally to purchase equipment, which is then leased to the business for its activities.

Additional Corporate Considerations

Up to this point, you've determined your tax consequences and the amount of capital you need to sustain both future growth and existing operations, and you've started the planning process. Now you must review some additional corporate issues.

Foremost among them is the issue of *business continuity*. The fiscal year-end process is the time to reexamine your business continuity arrangements. (The business continuity agreement, also called a buy-and-sell agreement, is the subject of Chapter 9.) Are your arrangements still appropriate? Are there additional owners or potential owners who should be included as part of the arrangement? Has the business increased in value?

If the value of your business has increased, do you need to consider an increase in the funding of a death or disability buyout? By reviewing business continuity arrangements, you and your advisors have an opportunity to make sure that your business objectives and goals are still consistent with each other. For example, continuity arrangements may require modification if one owner is more anxious to sell his interest, or retire, than the other.

Often the most valuable result of these fiscal year-end meetings is that business owners get the chance to discuss the problems they have with each other, or with the business, in the presence of impartial third parties who can offer suggestions and mediate differences.

A large part of my professional life is spent serving as a sounding board for a dissatisfied owner. Over the years I've found that like most of life's problems, those affecting relations between owners are best resolved at an early stage. Experienced advisors can help you and your partners resolve problems that may threaten your corporation.

Several years ago I helped structure a business buy-in for a young key employee. The intention was to have her eventually buy out an older majority shareholder's stock. As a result of the buy-in, the business prospered. In fact, it began growing too quickly for the older shareholder's comfort, and the younger shareholder grew concerned that she would have to pay the older shareholder for the increase in value.

Little was said between them, however, because they both

felt obligated to live up to the terms of their agreement. Instead, in their frustration and discomfort, they grew distant. Eventually they shared their feelings, separately, to one of the members of their advisory team. Thereafter it was a simple matter to redesign the buy-in to everyone's satisfaction and relief. We came up with a plan to accelerate the buy-in process while still giving the older owner a small piece of the future appreciation.

Issues and methods surrounding the transfer of your business interest to others is another critical part of ownership planning. Even if the idea of transferring your interest is only wishful thinking, it should be brainstormed at the year-end fiscal meeting, because that's where the process starts. Avoid the roadblocks to your eventual retirement by starting to plan early—and on the right path.

Business expansion or contraction is also considered yearly in connection with capital needs. If expansion appears likely, you and your advisors should consider banking and capital accumulation needs as well as the purchase of a larger building or the leasing of additional space. On the other hand, if contraction seems likely, your advisors can help you make difficult decisions to reduce your overhead. They may suggest layoffs, the sale of some equipment or other assets, a reduction in salaries, or other measures that may be too emotionally painful for you to undertake alone.

During a period of contraction, most businesses dig themselves into a deeper hole, not by cutting expenses too rapidly, but by hanging on too long to the existing operation, primarily because of pride or ego or a deep aversion to laying off loyal employees. Businesses also don't like to admit they are cutting back; the American way is to *grow, grow, grow.* Yet we've all seen businesses that spend themselves into bankruptcy. One of your most important goals must be to *preserve value* for the business in difficult times. Your advisory team demonstrates its greatest value when it helps you face hard facts and then helps you translate your decisions into action.

Employee considerations are another item for fiscal year-end review. I usually suggest that the business require key employees to sign contracts that restrict competition, protect trade secrets, and fully describe the compensation structure.

When owners balk at this, I point out some of the scenarios that could happen. This tends to change their thinking.

- A top salesman leaves and takes key accounts with him.
- A top manager leaves to start her own business with former employees.
- An employee who has access to key information about the company leaves, joins a competitor, and uses that information in a manner that hurts the business. (This information might include anything from a business plan to manufacturing secrets; pricing policies; or internally developed business forms, systems, methods, and procedures.)

Don't force yourself to learn only from your mistakes; keep in mind that employees are your primary means of making money. They are also your *primary means of losing money*. I approach the subject of employee agreements by asking, "If a particular employee left, what could he or she take that could damage the business?" The employment agreement is designed to prevent the employee from taking that valuable asset.

Sometimes such assurance is not possible and the risk must simply be borne. If so, plan to have other employees become involved in the same functions as the key employee. When he or she does leave, the business will be able to continue that key employee's work or function. You can then assure your key accounts that your service to them will continue uninterrupted.

The noncompete covenant is discussed in greater detail later in this chapter. Other, more pleasant employee considerations involve methods of motivating and retaining key employees. These are discussed in Chapter 3. Larger companies periodically review the issue of the unionization threat.

Compensation arrangements for key employees, in particular those whose compensation is not exclusively salary, is another important issue. Since your advisors represent hundreds of other closely held businesses, they can be a valuable source of information about salary levels, compensation structures, and, in general, what other businesses are doing to motivate and retain their key employees.

Again I urge you to extract as much information from your advisors as you can. That's what you're paying them for. *So come to the fiscal year-end meeting prepared with your own list of questions.* Make this meeting truly a vehicle to learn as much as you can.

Major business contracts and forms should be reviewed also, if not annually, at least on a periodic basis to make sure they remain current with state law and continue to protect your business. These include not only your sales invoice forms, but your space lease and bank loan documents. It is also advisable to review miscellaneous agreements, such as cafeteria plans, medical expense reimbursement plans, any leases you have with your business, and documents listed on the checklist in Exhibit 2-2.

A review or audit of your property, casualty, and liability policies is another wise step. This is normally done by a casualty insurance agent who typically does not attend fiscal year-end meetings. However, the agent should supply a written summary of your coverages for review at the meeting, enabling you and your advisors to detect any areas left uncovered by current policies. This can be critical not only to the profitability of your company, but to its very existence.

A case in point is what happened to one of my clients who sells heavy equipment. He had sold an item worth $200,000 and was storing it temporarily in a warehouse before delivery to the customer. A warehouse fire destroyed the equipment. My client's insurance covered only machinery "in transit"—not machinery in storage—and the warehouse owner's insurance covered only *his* building fixtures and equipment. My client suffered a $200,000 lick to his bottom line. Don't let this happen to you. Obtain a summary of your insurance coverage and have it reviewed by your advisory team at the year-end meeting.

Banking considerations are often reviewed at the fiscal year-end meeting. Your advisors normally know the local banks that are interested in working with your type of business. Your accountant should know whether your financial condition satisfies the lending requirements of your bank and its competitors, as well as whether the bank can meet your anticipated borrowing needs.

Frankly, it's darned hard to find a good bank for the closely held business owner. If you have one, keep it, even if you're paying a point more than might be necessary. If you don't have a good banking relationship, finding one should be a goal to be accomplished by the next planning meeting. Again, your advisors can help you locate, evaluate, and select a good bank for your business.

When you find miscellaneous other matters to review with your advisors, list them for attention later; the fiscal year-end meeting is the time to bring them up.

Individual Planning Considerations

The fiscal year-end meeting is also the right time to consider your *personal* planning—your individual income tax status, your financial planning, and your estate planning.

And right now is a good time to examine the issues involved in each area.

Your *individual income tax* status must be reviewed in conjunction with the business's tax status. The primary focus should be a balancing act between corporate and personal income taxes: Should the income be left in the company? Or taken out? A variety of techniques can then be used to reduce taxation at the individual level. These techniques are discussed in Chapter 11.

The fiscal year-end meeting presents an opportunity to coordinate the planning of your income taxes, both for the current year and for future years. Unlike businesses, individuals can't go back and recapture their past taxes. Therefore, it's important that you never pay more taxes than necessary.

Your company's fiscal year-end is also the time to look at

your *personal financial plan* to make sure it is consistent with your business and personal objectives. The financial plan, which is fully discussed in Chapter 10, shows you how to diversify and increase your assets. The meeting gives your financial planner access to information and ideas from your other advisors that will allow him to keep your plan current and coordinated with your business. He'll have the chance to ask your other advisors questions that will enable him to make the more accurate predictions and informed investment recommendations you'll need to meet your personal planning goals.

A good financial planner also recognizes the value of a team effort; he'll want to include your lawyer and accountant in that process, especially when you address estate planning considerations.

Much of a *business owner's estate* is tied up in the business—directly in the value of the business and indirectly in the income stream that builds up personal wealth and allows for payments of life insurance premiums. As your net worth increases, it may be necessary to make adjustments to your estate plan to reduce estate taxes. An estate plan is designed to attain certain objectives after your death, such as distribution of your assets, transfer of your business interest, education for your children, and income for your spouse and heirs (see Chapter 11).

For many owners this part of the fiscal year-end meeting requires almost no time at all. If their business has not increased much in value, their individual net worth remains unchanged—and if neither tax law nor their wishes have changed, this part of the meeting may be brief indeed. Nevertheless, reviewing the estate plan in the fiscal year-end meeting provides the chance to *reaffirm* that the plan is still the best plan for you.

Goal Setting

I often like to adjourn the fiscal year-end meeting at this point and reconvene at a local tavern or restaurant. I want the business owner to wind down from our formal meeting and to relax in a comfortable environment. To accomplish that, I announce I will not bill for this part of the meeting. That usually elicits an audible sigh of relief (and sometimes disbelief).

Once we get settled in a more leisurely atmosphere, I want to hear what the owner thinks about *the future of his business* as well as his own future in that business. I ask a lot of questions:

- Does the business opportunity look strong?
- What is his forecast for business revenues, sales, possible relocation.
- Is the business mature?
- How are the partners getting along?
- Is he pleased with his employees? His product mix? The advice and input he's getting from his advisors (including me)?
- What are his retirement plans? And timing?

Sometimes the answers I receive to these questions are no more than idle musings. Sometimes they are items fresh on the owner's mind and obviously well thought-out. In short, this informal part of the year-end meeting helps me find out where the owner wants to go and allows me and his other advisors to help him get there, a process that may take three, five, or ten years. The earlier we can embark on that venture, the more certain its success.

And that, after all, is the purpose of the fiscal year-end planning process—*to ensure the owner's success through planning, communication, and implementation.*

Speaking of implementation, a criticism many clients have of their lawyers is the failure to complete and return work on time. Whether it is an estate plan, a business contract, a buy-and-sell agreement, or a retirement plan, some lawyers seem to be habitual procrastinators. The fiscal year-end process can serve as an effective prod to your "bovine" attorney, or other advisors for that matter.

With all of your advisors present, you can establish a timetable to execute legal documents, implement financial planning products, and deliver income tax projections or financial statements. It's one thing for a lawyer to promise a client a document on time; it's quite another to make that promise in front of fellow advisors. Professional peer pressure can work in your behalf. If your attorney consistently fails to deliver documents on a timely basis—even under these circumstances—it is time to change law firms.

Another major problem with implementation is making the decision to turn words into actions. Suppose your financial planner suggests that your company buy additional life insurance for you. This might involve using a split-dollar agreement (essentially, a method of having the company pay the bulk of the premiums in exchange for the right to the cash value). Also, the accountant may want to do an analysis to ensure that the business can afford the additional premium, and your attorney may have an opinion regarding the overall impact of additional insurance on your estate plan.

If there is no meeting where all of this can be coordinated, the process of fact-finding among your advisors—and between them and you—can be time-consuming and costly. By reserving those decisions for the fiscal year-end meeting, when all your advisors are present, your decision making will be quick and less expensive.

Liability and Litigation

Although the legal audit can uncover potential problems and the fiscal year-end process can *prevent* problems, many situations exist where there is liability or litigation exposure. Potential situations you are likely to encounter in your daily business activities involve (1) employees, (2) customers and vendors, (3) the government, (4) the landlord, and (5) co-owners.

Employees

Based on what I've seen in the professional literature, the number of seminars that address the subject, and my own experiences with business owners, it seems certain one "hot stock" for the next ten years in litigation will be employee-employer relations.

I have already editorialized that one of the major reasons for the enormous number of lawsuits these days is that anyone who suffers an unpleasant experience, actual or perceived, thinks someone ought to pay him for it. Don't expect your employees to be the exception.

For hundreds of years, the fundamental tenet of employer-employee law was that of Employment at Will. This meant that the employee is hired at the will or whim of the boss and that the employee can be fired for any reason—or even no reason—without any recourse. In other words, *no one has a right to be employed.*

This principle has been eroded on several fronts.

First there was the historic rise of unionism, then employment safeguards were established in the federal civil services and other governmental employment systems. "Title VII" followed, giving government recourse and assistance to those who alleged discrimination in their employment on the basis of race, creed, color, nationality, age, or sex.

Still, until recently, a nonminority, private sector employee without an employment contract (collectively bargained or otherwise) could be fired for any reason or for no reason. Employment at Will as a concept seemed alive and well. In the last few years, however, that doctrine seems to have diminished in many parts of the country.

It appears that the courts have been striving to find some basis for avoiding the Employment at Will principle. They look to oral promises to the employee, employee manuals, or a course of conduct from which one could infer the existence of an enforceable employment contract that would eliminate the Employment at Will scenario.

To help protect against that possibility, it's vital that no promise of continued employment be found in your employee manual or your employee agreements. Obviously, you should not make such a promise orally or suggest it by your conduct. You should also take a proactive role in your relationship with your employees—that is, maintain appropriate records or, in former President Reagan's words, "Trust but verify."

Surprisingly, many closely held businesses neither keep employee files nor conduct periodic reviews of performance. The purpose of files is to know not only the employment history of a particular person, but to record any requests for corrective action in an employee's job performance.

Many employers don't care about documentation; courts and lawyers do. Lawyers always feel more comfortable firing someone if they can document that he or she has had the opportunity to correct faulty job behavior but failed to do so. This becomes all the more important if an employee falls within the scope of the Equal Employment Opportunity laws, for then you have the responsibility of proving you did not discriminate when you discharged the employee.

Wages are frequently a subject of dispute when an employee is let go. Without a written policy to the contrary, many employees feel they are entitled to be paid for any accumulated sick or vacation days upon their termination. However, a manual that clearly spells out your company policy on this matter is the best way to avoid any erroneous expectations.

As another example, if you have a history of giving two weeks' pay to "good" employees, who leave for reasons not connected with job performance, you may be establishing that right for all employees subsequently fired for poor performance. If you are inconsistent in this treatment—and your terminated employee takes you to court for failure to treat him as you've treated others—you might have to pay his attorney's fees and a penalty of 50 percent or more of the original amount owing, if that employee wins his suit. State laws on this vary.

You can see how easily this threat of litigation can coerce an employer into making payments to a fired employee when there are no clear-cut company directives governing employment termination.

Thus, many problems can be avoided with all employees by having a concise employee manual and personnel files, and by reaffirming, both in words and in conduct, that a contract for continued employment has not been created between the company and the employee. This curtails circumvention of the Employment at Will doctrine.

However, with key employees, even stronger medicine is required. I define a key employee as anyone who can harm the business upon his or her departure. With this employee more affirmative protection is necessary. One source of protection is the noncompete covenant. When I first discuss this with business owners, I invariably get two comments:

"They're not enforceable" is the first reaction.

Then, after reviewing what I've drawn up for them, they usually say, "If I were an employee, I would never sign this, so why should I expect my employees to sign it?"

My reply to the first comment is that in many states *covenants not to compete are, in fact, enforceable* if they involve key employees and the covenant is reasonable in scope, duration, and geographical territory. Obviously, you won't get much sympathy in court if your covenant goes overboard by, say, preventing a former employee from opening a competing business within five years anywhere in your state. I think two to three years is long enough to prevent your former employee from soliciting key accounts. And, generally, I don't like to see any geographical restriction; it's usually not necessary to protect your business.

I recommend that the scope of the covenant be as narrow as possible. In many sales-based organizations, for example, efforts to prevent a key sales manager from working within your metropolitan area may be unenforceable and probably are unnecessary. It may be important to make sure that the covenant prevents him from taking a sales line with him upon his departure. Or, perhaps, it's only important that he not be allowed to solicit your existing customers.

Determine *what is really important* if you lose your key employee. *Protect only that and no more.* Confine yourself to these objectives and your noncompete agreement is more likely to be enforceable. And you will be more comfortable asking your employee to sign it.

A second part of the employee contract should protect your trade secrets. Think of trade secrets as anything your business has created that makes it unique or more valuable. For a publisher it might be the subscriber list, for a sales organization a customer list, for a law firm its form files. You have a right—and a need—to legally prevent your business's information—its secrets—from being unwillingly shared with your competitors.

Customers and Vendors

To restate the obvious: Your customers are your life. They are your business opportunity.

Yet, because you are constantly dealing with them—your services or goods for their money—the potential for litigation is great. Recognizing the possibility of problems, most business owners (naturally) do absolutely nothing about it. They don't want to risk upsetting their customers with any written agreement setting forth the full terms and conditions of the sale—whether it be a simple sales invoice or an agreement covering the sale of services or equipment worth millions of dollars. They make a sales decision, not an ownership decision.

Indeed, there are many businesses that conduct million-dollar transactions daily over the telephone with no written contract of any kind. Trial lawyers want businesses to use this method—for obvious reasons. But lawyers who represent business owners prefer to have written contracts, or at least invoices with clearly defined terms (especially to provide for the payment of their client's attorney's fees in the event litigation or collection efforts are necessary).

Such lawyers also like written agreements because they tend to ensure that both sides have thought out the sales transaction, thus minimizing the potential for misunderstandings. These same lawyers like to see clauses in agreements that require arbitration or mediation before resorting to the courts.

Nonpayment of invoices is the most common reason for litigation with your customers. Usually, you will never receive payment even if you sue and win, because the business that you've sued doesn't have the money to pay (even though the owner may have sufficient assets). Consequently, it behooves you to make the personal guarantee of the business owner part of your standard business form.

Much of what we've reviewed here about customers also applies, in reverse, to your relationship with your suppliers. I recently counseled one of our clients whose business was failing. We looked at the total debt of his business, which amounted to $750,000. We next examined the total business assets available to pay that debt. They amounted to $400,000. Finally, we calculated the total amount of business debt he had *personally guaranteed*—$550,000.

After first reviewing and complying with the fraudulent conveyance laws and bankruptcy preference laws, guess which obligations we suggested he pay from the business assets?

This example illustrates why, as a creditor, you always want a personal guarantee, and why, as a business debtor, you never want to sign a personal guarantee. If you are forced to sign one, at least negotiate to have it automatically lapse if you are current with a creditor after a short period of time—about one year or so. Most standard invoices and sales agreements do not contain language for a personal guarantee—so be sure your lawyer drafts one for your invoices.

Government

Just as you need your customer's money, Uncle Sam needs yours. There are differences, however.

Because your customer can usually go elsewhere, you must provide a good product and service, a fair price and—to avoid disputes and problems—clear communication with your customer. If a misunderstanding arises, you should be quick to nip it in the bud and resolve your differences amicably.

The government, however, doesn't care about interpersonal relations. Mediation, conciliation, and compromise are generally incompatible with a strict interpretation and enforcement of rules and regulations. Because of the super abundance of such rules and regulations, it's virtually impossible for you to know all of them, much less comply with all of them. Instead, you hire advisors who have the knowledge. That's why the legal audit and fiscal year-end planning process are invaluable as tools to prevent problems from arising. This is often a place where prevention is crucial, a cure impossible.

The Landlord

If you lease space for your business, you undoubtedly signed a lengthy form submitted to you by your landlord. I can promise you that the legal-sized, thirty-plus-page, single-spaced, two-sided document contains not one sentence favorable to you, the tenant.

In most situations the lease is of long-term duration and represents by far the most significant financial obligation of your business (and for you, as well, since without your lawyer's help you may have been forced to guarantee its performance). Once again, the best method of minimizing your exposure is to plan ahead by having experienced counsel review and negotiate the proposed new lease well before the existing lease expires.

As of this writing, many parts of the country have seen an overbuilding of all kinds of commercial structures. It's a renter's market. Consequently, there is a tremendous amount of negotiating room available if you will only take advantage of it. Even if you have a limited legal budget, I suggest that this be one item you not scrimp on. Too much is at stake.

The Co-Owners

Many years ago our law firm decided it was poor business practice to handle divorce cases. Little did we know that divorce wouldn't go away but simply take another form—dealing with business co-owners who don't get along with each other. The only difference between the two types of divorce practices is that we are not concerned with child support and custody when dealing with business co-owners (although we often seem to be dealing with childlike behavior).

Like marital divorces that are much easier to settle when there is a premarital or postmarital agreement, business divorces are easier where there is a buy-and-sell agreement. The existence of this document serves to prevent undue economic and emotional harm in the event of a business split-up.

In the case of multiple ownership, I also suggest employment agreements for each owner. These agreements should describe not only the compensation, but also the duties to be performed by each. Because disputes do arise between co-owners, don't hesitate to use your advisors as intermediaries if you are reluctant to directly confront your business partner. Again, this can be a valuable adjunct to the fiscal year-end planning session.

Summary

Most litigation between business owners and their employees, customers, vendors, and co-owners results not from fraud or deception by one side, but from failure to communicate, to understand, and to think through all of the possibilities.

An important reason to conduct a legal audit is to review how you document your business relationships. When your lawyer makes a suggestion to improve your documentation, think hard about implementing it. Don't wait until you've suffered losses that could have been prevented. The fiscal year-end meeting continues the communication process—communication between co-owners and their advisors that serves to prevent problems.

Finally, think hard also about your relationships with co-owners, customers, vendors, the government, and your landlord to make sure they don't become the roadblocks to your success.

LEGAL AUDIT CHECKLIST

The exhibits on fiscal year-end meetings and the legal audit serve as a good checklist for accomplishing the objectives of this chapter. In addition, you should assemble all legal documents used in your business and indicate when they were last reviewed or revised. The following list will help make certain that you have either signed originals of any documents requiring a signature, or photocopies of signed documents.

	Last Date
Description	*Revised or Reviewed*
☐ Partnership agreement	_____
☐ Corporate documents	
1. Articles of incorporation	_____
2. Bylaws	_____
3. Minutes	_____
4. Wage continuation plan	_____
5. Medical reimbursement plan	_____
6. Stock certificates	_____
7. Subchapter S election	_____
8. Incentive stock option plan	_____
9. Nonqualified stock option plan	_____
☐ Change of registered office/agent	_____
☐ Employment agreements for owners	_____
☐ Employment agreements for employees	_____
☐ Trade secrecy/covenant not to compete agreements	_____
☐ Buy/sell agreements	_____
☐ Deferred compensation plan	_____
☐ Office and facility leases	_____
☐ Equipment leases	_____
☐ Authority to do business in other states	_____
☐ Bonus plans	_____
☐ Loan agreement with banks, other lenders, and between the company and owners	_____

- ☐ Guaranty and indemnity agreements   _____
- ☐ Contracts and other agreements with third   _____
  parties including invoices
- ☐ Qualified retirement plans
  1. Profit sharing   _____
  2. Money purchase   _____
  3. 401(k)   _____
  4. Defined benefit plan   _____
  5. ESOP   _____
- ☐ Split dollar agreements   _____
- ☐ Purchase agreements for original   _____
  acquisition of business
- ☐ Other   _____

Finally, assemble an advisory team of attorney, accountant, and financial planner/insurance agent who are proactive rather than reactive. Arrange for your tentative advisory team to meet with you over lunch or after work. There should be no charge for this. The purpose is to determine mutual goals and objectives for you and your business—the three objectives discussed in this book. This is the time for the advisors to become acquainted with one another and to be sure that they are compatible rather than competitive. Encourage each of your advisors to read this book in order for them to help understand the role they are to play in achieving your owner objectives, but make sure that they don't charge you for reading.

3

How to Motivate and Keep Key Employees

Creating value in your business through staff

The one indispensable component of a valuable business is its top employees. So when you ask yourself, "What is the most effective way to *create* and *build* value in my business?" the correct answer is "Finding, keeping, and motivating key employees." There are two important reasons:

1. Truly good key employees *do* increase the value of your business.
2. They often become potential owners when you decide to retire or move on to another venture.

What are you doing to motivate your key employees so that they will want to remain with your company? Obviously you have provided a reward system that begins with a salary and, perhaps, offers something else. The question is, Is it the best one? How do you evaluate the system you now have in place? There are a variety of incentive packages from which you can choose—packages designed to help your key employees obtain their financial and psychic goals. When your key employees attain *their* goals, you will achieve *your* ownership goal of building value and eventually converting that value into money.

The Key Employee

Before we discuss specific measures, we need to distinguish between the majority of your employees and those we've termed *key* employees.

Most of your employees are attracted and motivated by the usual items—a pleasant work environment, a stimulating job, good wages and benefits, and job security. The really *key* people want more. They think and act more like you. They are eager to be given responsibilities and challenges. Like you, they want to see the business grow and prosper, and they want to grow and prosper along with it. They take pride in being identified with, and contributing to, a successful business. In short, they *act* like an owner.

Identifying these unique employees and nurturing their desires is like nurturing your own. The end result can only serve to increase the worth of the business.

The Purpose of Incentive Packages

Good business owners are interested in more than simply motivating their key employee; the owner also wants to retain that employee. The advantages of motivating and retaining key employees are many. Initially, there is the obvious one of making the business more profitable. This is where most business owners stop thinking; this is where you must begin. A stable, motivated management is an asset that potential purchasers will pay a lot of money for. Further, this same key employee, or group of key employees, is also the most likely candidate to purchase your business when you reach retirement age, or your second childhood, and you decide to try something else.

There are several aspects of providing incentives for retaining and motivating key employees. At the outset one overriding principle must be mentioned. As we say out here in Colorado, "Don't bet the ranch on the best-looking horse."

True, all business owners make mistakes, especially concerning personnel. And reading this book won't prevent you from doing so, anymore than writing it will ensure that I never again make a mistake in hiring or promoting my own employees. But if handled properly, these mistakes should be no more than temporary setbacks to the business. However, if you have promised or given an employee stock or some other nonforfeitable right and you lack the means to retrieve that stock, you have made a costly mistake—one that may permanently affect the future course of your business.

Contrary to the stereotype of a business owner as miserly and condescending, almost all *successful* owners are, in fact, characterized by a spirit of generosity and a desire to be liked by their employees. Your business is a major part of your life, and you want to feel good when you interact with your fellow workers. Thus, a fundamental element in key employee arrangements is protecting you from your own generosity, especially when it is misplaced.

Simply installing key employee incentive documents will not ensure success in motivating and retaining your key employees. Managerial and leadership talent must also be present. Likewise, having the talent is insufficient without a carefully planned, documented, and implemented incentive program that is specific to the needs of your business.

Such a plan will have certain basic characteristics:

1. It will reward the key employees by being *financially attractive*, rewarding the key employees when they achieve certain high, but attainable, performance standards; it will be determinable in specific dollar amounts and given on at least a yearly basis.
2. By vesting the reward—linking payment to tenure—you encourage the employee to remain on the job in order to receive the reward. Sometimes called "golden

handcuffs,'' the *vested* reward may be in the form of an ownership interest or compensation that is deferred until a specific future event.

3. Even good plans fail when there is ineffective communication. To be successful, any incentive arrangement you offer must be thoroughly *understood* by your key employee; the plan must be in writing and, if complicated, must contain a written summary that is easy to read. To ensure that a plan is understood, conduct a face-to-face meeting with your key employee so that you or your advisors can explain it and answer questions.

Stock or Cash-Based Bonus?

Although there are many ways to provide incentives, most owners offer either stock or a cash-based bonus. Both methods are strong stimulants for key employees and can be used effectively to motivate them to perform well and remain on the job in order to achieve their personal goals of job security, job satisfaction, and a pot of gold at the end of the rainbow.

Before I tell you how and why you should issue stock to key employees, let me tell you why you *should not: All too often, issuing stock to employees makes litigation lawyers wealthy. And this author—also a lawyer—doesn't like litigation lawyers messing with his clients!* But that's beside the point. The main issue is this: Strange things can happen when you decide to give some stock to that invaluable key employee. Take the case of Centennial Contractors, Inc.

Not long ago I met with three talented, hardworking owners of a contracting business. Starting from scratch, they had built up the business to the point where it had a book value of more than a half million dollars. Each of the partners owned 30 percent of the company, and they regarded each other as being equally valuable to the organization. The problem was that they had a fourth owner.

Shortly after founding the company, they had given an employee, Jim Jakeaway, a 10 percent share of the company because they felt he was one of the best estimators in the industry. Indeed, he proved to be a tremendous estimator. Unfortunately, as the business grew, a problem surfaced: No one was willing to work under him. His personality was so abrasive that he was incapable of managing what became the estimating department. He also refused to work under anyone else. The only alternative was to let him go.

When the majority owners told him he was being discharged, he reminded them that he owned 10 percent of the company. "What are you going to do about that?" he asked. The other owners belatedly realized that there was no buy-back agreement to require Jakeaway to resell his stock upon termination. Since he paid nothing for the stock, he had little incentive to sell it. He had the three majority owners over a barrel, and he knew it.

After the meeting Jakeaway went to his lawyer and learned that, as a minority shareholder, he was entitled to attend all shareholder meetings and to review the company books and records—including the financial data of the company—at any reasonable time. By nature Jakeaway was prickly. He felt he had been wronged by the other owners, who did not fully appreciate his qualities. He felt humiliated at being fired when he considered himself an equal owner with the other owners. In short, he wanted his pound of flesh—and he got it. Eventually the three majority owners settled for a cash payment of $100,000—more than half of the company's taxable income for that year.

This example illustrates several typical problems encountered by the owners of closely held businesses.

1. The majority owners offered stock ownership to someone to whom they probably did not *have* to offer ownership. A simple cash bonus plan based upon the company's profitability probably would have been a sufficient incentive.
2. The owners made no provision to buy back the stock in the event things turned sour.
3. There was no mechanism for fixing the value of the stock in the event of a repurchase.

4. They were totally ignorant of the substantial rights that a minority shareholder has in a corporation.
5. They made a mistake when they thought Jakeaway was a long-term key employee. When the business was grossing $500,000, he was important; when the revenues grew to $5 million, however, he was no longer critical to its success. Indeed, he had become a hindrance.

The majority owners had good intentions when they offered Jakeaway a small ownership interest in the company. But their plan backfired. Instead of benefiting from the capable services of an outstanding estimator for many years, they had to fire him. In the process they learned a lot about "rights" and "obligations"—the rights of minority shareholders, the obligations that majority shareholders have toward a minority owner, and the rights of disclosure enjoyed by all shareholders.

Think about this: When you relinquish any ownership in your business—even one share out of a million—you unwittingly give the new shareholder substantial legal rights. The changes in the company's operations can be the difference between benevolent despotism and democracy. Even an inconsequential minority shareholder has certain statutory rights such as the right to be informed about the financial condition of the company and often a right to be consulted and given the opportunity to vote on major decisions of the company. Further, majority shareholders have a duty to deal fairly with minority shareholders, and as directors they have a duty of due care and loyalty to the company which can be used by minority shareholders to attack any self-serving actions, real or apparent. For example, a majority owner may think he has the right to drive a company car—and selects a Mercedes Benz. However, a minority owner could allege the majority owner was disregarding his duty of exercising due care for the welfare of the company—that a Ford Escort would be a more appropriate vehicle!

Thus, issuance of stock—even a small amount—gives the

shareholder a right that is far greater than merely sharing in the growth of the company. With forethought the problems associated with these rights can be limited or even eliminated.

Two other interesting phenomena—one intended, the other unintended—can occur when stock is given to a key employee.

First, the image that an employee has of her role in the company can suddenly change. Now she is an owner and concludes that her status relative to her co-workers has been raised. She becomes more loyal, more motivated, more eager to see the profits of the company increase in order to expand the value of her stock. That's exactly what you hoped would happen.

However, that employee's colleagues may become jealous, apprehensive, or resentful. Until now they had seen themselves as her equals. Suddenly she has acquired new status. Soon they are demanding ownership in the company as well. Failing to get it, they may quit their jobs or become so disruptive they must be fired. In attempting to reward a key employee, you have inadvertently antagonized other competent and potentially key employees.

The moral? Don't shoot yourself in the foot. Consider the ripple effect on those not included in the incentive program before your magnanimity threatens your company's success.

Does the above example mean that owners should never offer stock in their companies to key employees? I have to answer with my favorite lawyerlike response, "It depends." Circumstances will determine whether this is the right incentive for the situation.

The best time to award stock to a valued key employee is when all three of the following conditions are present:

1. You have identified a key employee or group of employees who have been with your company at least two years.
2. The key employee or employees would be more motivated by receiving stock than cash.

3. You are prepared to award the employee or employees a *meaningful* amount of stock.

Having listed these conditions, I now offer some words of caution.

Suppose you decide to offer stock because you have insufficient cash flow to offer money as a reward? It's seldom a good idea to give stock to an employee who prefers cash; he'll only want to convert the stock to cash anyway, perhaps by quitting. Moreover, as we shall see, there are ways to provide for a deferred cash incentive that would be more attractive to such employees than stock would be.

In condition No. 3, I use the word *meaningful* advisedly; nothing is worse than offering an incentive award the recipient regards as inadequate. I learned this the hard way when my partner and I offered a small ownership interest to one of our key employees. We thought the offer generous; he perceived it otherwise because he expected to be offered five times as much! Looking back, we realized we had neglected to discuss with him *his* expectations. We also failed to describe how additional stock ownership could be acquired based on *future performance*. We lost an excellent employee who became a respected competitor.

In short, if you are unable or unwilling to make a substantial commitment of stock ownership to a key employee, make certain the lesser amount will be perfectly acceptable before you make the offer; otherwise, consider cash or deferred compensation as an alternative compensation package.

Unquestionably, providing the opportunity for stock ownership is the most powerful motivating—and retaining—factor a closely held business can offer a top employee. For that reason it can often backfire for the majority owners if the employee's expectations are frustrated, and it can serve as a powerful disincentive to your key employee if not planned carefully.

I recall the time I met with Nels Olinger, the owner of an engine rebuilding business he had started twenty years earlier.

Nels wanted to begin the transfer of stock to his son, who had already taken over the operations. In the ensuing conversation, I learned that soon after he formed his company Nels had given 10 percent of the stock to his secretary, Anna. And he had made no provision to repurchase the stock when she left the company.

Five years after receiving the stock, Anna quit. When we tracked her down, she was able to produce her stock certificate. After considerable negotiation she agreed to sell her stock back to the company at 10 percent of the current book value of the company. That came to $30,000. Had she been less friendly, the damage could have been far greater. Still, it wasn't easy for Nels to pay the $30,000 to an employee who hadn't worked for him in fifteen years. He estimated that amount probably equaled her earnings during her entire term of employment with the company. Moreover, it reduced Nels's retirement fund by that amount because there was that much less money available from the company to pay him for his stock.

In retrospect it was a careless transfer of stock to a good employee, but certainly not a key employee; Anna could not substantially increase the overall profitability or worth of the business. In addition Nels's generous gesture was made without any consideration of what it would cost him to reacquire the stock after it appreciated in value. And, finally, it even failed as an incentive to motivate and keep Anna as an employee.

So far I've bombarded you with tales of unsuccessful stock incentive plans. So many plans fail, I believe, because of one or more of the following reasons:

• The plan is not directed toward any of the three proper business objectives of owners—to increase the value of the owner's stock, to eventually transfer his stock to another for maximum profit, and to integrate his business ownership with his personal income, estate, and financial planning. Transferring stock to a key employee must accomplish one of these three objectives if it is to be ultimately successful.

• Stock is given to the wrong person, often someone who joined the company in its early years but whose importance to the company diminishes as it grows.

• The stock plan is incomplete. It contains deficiencies. For example, if no method is provided by which the receiving employee can obtain additional stock (or, at a minimum, receive periodic notices of changes in the stock's value), the employee will eventually come to view the stock as a reward for past performance, rather than an incentive for future performance.

• Communication is poor. The key employee never really understands the purpose, terms, and conditions of the plan. As a result, the plan not only fails as an incentive; it actually becomes a *disincentive* because owner and employee do not have identical expectations.

• A "damage control instrument" is missing. Even the best-laid plans can go wrong and your key employee may leave for any reason. At that time you need a buy-back agreement that obligates the employee to sell his stock back to you at a predetermined price and upon predetermined terms.

When implemented correctly, however, a carefully designed stock incentive plan can help the owner achieve his three business goals:

1. Increase the value of the company by motivating and retaining a key employee or group of employees.
2. Generate an individual or group of individuals who ultimately purchase the owner's stock.
3. Integrate his business ownership with his personal income, estate, and financial planning by selling his stock directly to a key employee or employees.

Thus, careful planning can—and does—produce successful results when stock incentives are employed correctly. Take the case of Lindsay Mining, International (LMI).

LMI was an international mining company based in Australia. It had established a United States subsidiary in Colorado with offices in several other states. To attract and keep the best talent in the industry, it had to offer more than high salaries. LMI soon discovered it needed to offer ownership, financial incentives, and some form of "golden handcuffs."

Over the years, LMI provided bonuses of stock in the U.S. subsidiary to its American managers, a small group ranging from three to six individuals. The company also provided a cash bonus plan based on the annual profits of the U.S. subsidiary. The stock and cash bonuses were rewards for that year's performance.

Because of the company's financial success and the valuation formula for its stock, the American managers enjoyed current cash bonuses as well as substantial growth in the value of their ownership interests. Moreover, LMI had a *written* plan that *required* the company to issue additional shares of stock to the key managers if certain increases in the value of the American subsidiary were attained. These "performance standards" were realistic, achievable through strong effort, and determinable.

By their actions the American managers were able to increase their personal wealth while simultaneously increasing the overall wealth of the business enterprise. Everyone benefited.

This plan worked because it suffered none of the weaknesses described earlier. Later, one key employee of LMI left the business upon the request of the other key managers. His stock was repurchased according to a fixed formula with a fixed payout. His employment agreement also provided for a fixed severance payment amount.

By having everything in black and white, both sides knew the exact cost of that person's departure. The damage control instrument worked, and at this printing the business was stronger than ever.

How to Transfer Stock to Key Employees

Once you've determined that stock is an appropriate incentive package for that favored employee or employees, how do you go about awarding it? There are two principal ways, each with its variations and peculiar tax and control consequences. Let's review each method.

Issuing Stock

Stock can be issued to an employee either through a "nonqualified stock bonus" or by allowing him to purchase the stock at either its fair market value or a discounted price.

With the nonqualified stock bonus, the employee receives stock from the company. The fair market value of the stock is determined and the value of that stock is taxable to the employee as ordinary income in the year he receives it. The company receives an income tax deduction for the value of the stock given to the employee. Thus, if you decide to have the company issue 100 shares to a key employee, and each share of stock is worth $500, the employee's income increases by $50,000 and the corporation deducts $50,000.

The primary benefit to the key employee, in addition to acquiring stock worth $50,000, is growth in the value of the stock, which directly benefits the owner as well.

Typically, a stock bonus is part of a formal stock bonus plan. The plan fixes how much stock the employee is to be issued on an annual basis—for example, $5,000 worth of stock per year for five years. The plan also provides a formula for valuing and repurchasing the stock. Then, if the employee later leaves, the stock would be repurchased by the employer. If the stock increased in value while held by the employee, he would be able to realize its value from the sale of the stock back to the corporation.

Finally, incentives should be built into the plan so that stock is given only upon the attainment of defined performance goals, such as a profit amount, revenue increase, or some other measurable fiscal event. There must also be a written agreement requiring the repurchase of the stock upon the employee's termination of employment for any reason at an agreed-upon formula to determine price per share.

Purchasing the stock with a cash bonus is another way a key employee can acquire stock from the corporation or from other key employees, including you. If the stock is purchased at less than fair market value, then the employee will have taxable income on the difference between the fair market value of the stock and the price actually paid, and the company will have an offsetting deduction.

This concept is similar to the stock bonus plan, except that it often gives the key employee an option to select cash or stock. For example, each year a key employee may be given 2 percent of the net profits payable in cash or by stock of equivalent value. Again, the value of whatever the employee receives is taxable income to him and is an offsetting deduction for the company.

This method gives the employee a bit more flexibility than the standard stock bonus; if he needs cash in a particular year, it is available to him instead of stock. And some employees, even key employees, will often have such a need for cash that offering the option of a cash bonus for superior performance is of overriding importance.

Stock Options

Stock options can be separated into two types—qualified and nonqualified. The former is known as an incentive stock option (ISO), and like qualified retirement plans, it is a creature of the tax code. With both types the key employee is given the right to purchase stock at a given price. With the ISO, the price must be no less than the fair market value at the date the option is first granted. The option, which is granted for a specific time period not to exceed ten years, is exercised when the employee pays money and receives stock in return.

The primary tax difference between the two types of stock options are the tax consequences, both to the company and to the employee. Under a nonqualified stock option, the difference between the amount paid by the employee when the option is exercised and the then-current fair market value of the stock is taxable as ordinary income to the employee and is deducted by the corporation. With an ISO there are ordinarily no tax consequences to either the employee or the corporation when the option is granted or exercised by the employee. Instead, if certain holding periods are observed, when the stock is ultimately sold back to the corporation by the employee, he recognizes capital gain on the difference between the sale price and price paid when the option was exercised. As is the case whenever a corporation buys its own stock, there is no tax deduction to the company.

Consider the case of Ken Brown, which follows, to witness how a typical incentive stock option plan works.

A Typical Stock Option

Let's suppose that the Acme Corporation offers Ken Brown, a key employee, an option to buy 100 shares of stock for $500 per share. The employee is not allowed to exercise the option unless Acme's cumulative profits exceed $500,000. The previous year's profits were $250,000. Once the company reaches $500,000, Brown has three years to exercise part or all of the option. The benchmark is reached two years later, and Brown is eligible to exercise the option a year later. However, he decides to wait until the last year of the option period because it does him no good to exercise his option before he needs to. By holding the option, he has been able to see the value of the shares of stock increase from $500 per share, under the formula originally used, to over $1,200 per share five years later.

If Brown leaves Acme at any time before he is entitled to exercise the stock option, he forfeits the option. If he leaves after he is entitled to buy the stock, but before he has actually done so, the plan provides that he is entitled to the "gain" on the stock—even though he did not actually purchase it. If he leaves after he has purchased the stock, the stock is automatically repurchased by the corporation.

An incentive stock option plan can also be tied into a cash bonus plan in which the corporation gives the employee a bonus equal to the purchase price for the stock when the option is exercised. It works like this:

Suppose the total cost of Brown's option is $50,000. The company pays Brown a bonus of $50,000, for which it gets a tax deduction. Brown adds the $50,000 to his taxable income. Now Brown returns the $50,000 to his company in exchange for the stock. The company pays no tax on the sale of its stock. At this point the corporation has received an income tax deduction of $50,000, yet it is out no cash because it has received the $50,000 back tax free for the sale of its stock. Brown is out only the tax cost of the bonus.

From the employee's standpoint, this is a small cost indeed when the fair market value of the stock has increased substantially since the date of the offer. Like an ISO, however, or any other redemption of stock, the company will repurchase the stock with after-tax dollars.

In sum, the stock option offers more flexibility than does the stock bonus, and thus more planning opportunity for the owner and key employee. Stock options provide the added benefit of giving the key employee growth opportunities from the beginning without the need to pay money or even incur a current tax cost. Further, until the option is exercised, he does not participate as a shareholder and has no shareholder rights.

Keep in mind that stock carries with it three characteristics. One, it reflects the equity—the value—of the company. As the company grows in value, the value of the stock grows proportionately. Two, stock ownership can mean voting—controlling the company. This latter factor is variable, and nonvoting stock can be issued. And three, stock ownership means having general shareholder rights, such as the privilege of examining books and records and attending meetings.

Retaining Key Employees Without Giving Up Stock Ownership

There are, of course, ways to provide key employees with attractive incentives that don't involve the risk associated with stock ownership. These methods can even give rights to appreciation in stock without actually offering stock.

There are three primary nonstock incentive plans: (1) the cash bonus plan, (2) the Stock Appreciation Rights (SAR) plan, and (3) the nonqualified deferred compensation plan.

The Cash Bonus Plan

With the cash bonus plan, the business owner simply promises to pay an amount of money, perhaps a flat amount or a percentage of the company's annual profits, if the key employee attains some measurable goal. The goal might be an increase in revenues or profitability within his department, or an overall increase in the company's profitability.

The advantages of this plan are that it is easily understood, cash is always welcome and appreciated, and the bonus is generally rewarded shortly after the goal is achieved. The only disadvantages to the owner are that it requires an actual outlay of cash and that it presents no "strings"—that is, the reward is given outright, rather than being paid at some future date and thereby tying your top employees to your company.

Stock Appreciation Rights

A more useful incentive to persuade the key employees to remain is the Stock Appreciation Rights (SAR) plan. Tied to the employees' performance, the SAR plan gives them some of the benefits of stock ownership without requiring that they acquire any.

Typically, units corresponding to shares of stock—but not representing any actual ownership—are allocated to the participating employees and credited on the business's books and records. An account is set up and maintained for each key employee. Since key employees don't actually own the stock, they have no shareholder rights; however, each unit appreciates in value as the value of the stock increases. Any dividends paid on the stock—as well as other changes in the capital structure—are credited to the employee's account.

When the employee leaves the company, the units in his account are reevaluated to reflect the current market price, or formula price of the stock. Depending on how the employer designs the plan, the employee receives his benefit in a lump sum at the time of departure or in a series of payments over several years. Thus, he benefits from stock appreciation even though none was ever issued to him.

Compared with actual stock ownership, SAR plans offer certain advantages.

For participating employees:

- No initial investment is required.
- Additional income may be deferred.

For employers:

- Benefits are tax-deductible.
- There is no need to draft stock repurchase agreements.
- Employees are not granted rights to vote, inspect books, or attend meetings.
- SAR plans may be tied to vesting requirements.

The last advantage may be especially appealing to the business owner because he can design the plan so that the key employee's full right to an SAR is vested over a period of years, perhaps at the rate of 10 percent per year. For example, suppose a key employee is given an SAR in 100 units having a current value of $50 each, or a total of $5,000, subject to vesting at the rate of 10 percent a year. Then the employee leaves four years later when each unit is worth $100. Instead of receiving $50 per unit—the total amount of the appreciation—the employee would receive only $20 per unit, 40 percent of the total appreciation. This exemplifies the "golden handcuffs" approach that is so important in retaining key employees.

The chief elements of SAR plans are *vesting, forfeiture, payment schedules, and funding devices.* These are also common in deferred compensation plans, which also include *benefit formulas.* However, in SAR plans, the benefit formula is not included because the stock appreciation element *is* the benefit formula.

The Nonqualified Deferred Compensation Plan

Another alternative is the use of nonqualified deferred compensation—a promise by the business to pay an employee at a future date for his current or future services. The use of this form of executive compensation has increased markedly in recent years.

Its primary benefit to the business is that these essentially private retirement plans don't have to meet funding, employee coverage, or most other requirements of "qualified" retirement plans, thereby reducing the cost to the business. Also, the plan can become a golden handcuff by adding certain restrictions on how the key employee exercises his rights to the compensation.

A primary benefit to your key employee is that he receives no taxable income until the date when he becomes entitled to the deferred compensation amounts. The income tax issues connected with deferred compensation are reviewed in Chapter 4.

Deferred compensation arrangements can be structured in many ways, but all will have in common the elements of benefit formula, vesting, forfeiture, payment schedules, and funding devices.

Let's look at each.

Benefit Formula: There are several types of benefit formuals, such as a *defined benefit* formula where the company agrees to pay a definite amount at some point in the future, or a *defined contribution* approach where the company promises to credit a specified amount to a bookkeeping account on a regular basis.

A third approach, especially useful for retaining key employees, is an *incentive compensation* formula. Here, the business promises to pay to a key employee an amount equal to the value of his deferred compensation account at the time benefits become payable. The amount credited to the account is based on stated employee performance standards. This helps to encourage employee productivity. If the performance standards are selected carefully, the business's liability to fund the plan exists typically only when the company is profitable.

Vesting: Provides motivation for employees to stay with the company in order to become entitled to all of the benefits that have accrued to them under the benefit formula. Unlike qualified retirement plans, there is no limit on the length of any vesting schedule. If a plan has no vesting requirement, then your key employee has the right to 100 percent of whatever benefits he is entitled to whenever he quits.

"One-time vesting" is a simple schedule that after a specified number of years of continuous employment vests all rights to the deferred compensation in the employee. A key employee, for example, may be vested at the rate of 10 percent a year in his deferred compensation account balance. After 10 years of employment, the employee would be 100 percent vested as to all amounts in the plan when he terminates employment.

A second type of vesting is called "continual vesting." This is a single vesting schedule that is applied separately to each year's contribution. Since each year is treated separately—again, perhaps at 10 percent annual vesting rate—the employee will never be completely vested in every year's contribution until the vesting requirement lapses, generally when the employee reaches retirement age.

Forfeiture: Allows an owner to terminate an employee's vested rights. This is another device for influencing your key employee's behavior. For instance, forfeiture can be used to reclaim some or all of an employee's vested benefits if he leaves your business and violates his employment agreement, which may include a covenant not to compete nor to disclose proprietary information. This gives your former employee, who also may know many of your trade secrets, an added incentive to honor the promises he made in the employment agreement.

Payment Schedules: The deferred compensation agreement should contain payment schedules, that is, provisions that determine when payments begin and how long they are to be continued after the employee leaves.

Funding Devices: There are methods available to provide a pool of funds that the employer may draw upon to pay deferred compensation without subjecting the employee to a risk of current taxation. A funding device also provides psychological security for the employee, who then knows the monies will be there when he becomes eligible to receive them, and thus makes it easier to sell the plan to him. Many plans are unfunded, although ordinarily I urge my clients to begin a safe investment plan, such as investing in permanent cash value life insurance products at the corporate level.

When Nonstock Plans Work Best

Given the choice, almost all key employees would prefer stock ownership over nonstock arrangements. However, nonstock incentive arrangements should be considered when issuing stock is not a good alternative. Nonstock incentives work best in situations where there are key employees within a family-owned-and-operated business, and where it is evident that the younger generation of that family will eventually own the company. In these situations something should be done to retain key employees.

Naturally, this reminds me of a client—the Thomas Wells Construction Company.

Tom Wells had started the company more than forty years before we met. It had grown to annual revenues of almost $30 million. Although Wells had done extensive family transition planning, he knew that as he stepped back from the business and allowed his son to take over its management and control he would need the active and intense involvement of his key personnel.

This group consisted of three construction foremen, the overall operations manager, and the chief financial officer. While Wells remained active, he knew he would be able to replace the loss of one or more of these key managers; however, Wells felt that his relatively inexperienced son needed time to gain further experience. Thus, it made sense to keep the current management team in place.

But what kind of incentive arrangement would be appropriate

to keep them on the job? Issuing stock or stock options was not an alternative, since Wells intended that the business remain firmly in the hands of the family.

As we talked, I learned that Wells had historically given cash bonuses as a reward in profitable years. Given the nature of the construction business, it was not unusual for the company to make $500,000 one year and lose $200,000 the next. This history of cash bonuses seemed an appropriate concept to build upon, because everybody was already familiar with it.

We also knew that, as the business grew, additional key people would be hired. They, too, should be given an opportunity to participate in any incentive plan. The plan we devised followed the necessary elements of any well-designed incentive plan.

It offered a *substantial benefit*—25 percent of the after-tax profits on an annual basis was available to the group of key employees. Forty percent of this amount would be distributed outright to the participants under the incentive plan. The remaining 60 percent would go as a credit into the accounts of each of the five key employees.

As additional key employees were added to the plan, they would share in the overall 25 percent profit, which would be distributed among the participants as determined by a management committee of three people. The committee consisted of one member of the Wells family and two members of the key employee group.

There was a compelling *incentive* to remain a productive employee of the company. A 15-year continual vesting schedule was attached to the deferred benefit; it would take 15 years for each key employee to become fully vested in each year's contribution. However, upon attaining age 58, the employees would be 100 percent vested in all amounts allocated to their benefit. All of this was contained in a well-designed *written plan*.

The key management also had the ability to control—to some degree—the amount of their deferred compensation, because their performance directly affected the profitability of the company— another powerful *incentive* to consistently do well.

The plan was carefully *explained* to all members over a series of meetings attended by Tom Wells, his son, us and the accountants, and all of the participants.

The plan has worked out well for all concerned.

Summary

You probably have employees in your company who are vital to its success. Providing these key employees with an incentive package that motivates them to continue to excel and to remain with you is in your best interest. These key employees not only will make your business more profitable, but will most likely be strong candidates to buy it should you choose to sell it. Your immediate task is to identify these key employees, find the right incentive package, and implement it.

Now is the time to take a hard look at your current employee benefit programs, especially those aimed at your key employees. Ask yourself the questions listed in the Employee Benefit Checklist. Make sure you include such programs as group health, disability, life, "cafeteria programs," qualified retirement plans, cash bonus plans, and any others.

EMPLOYEE BENEFIT CHECKLIST

☐ Do any of these plans favor a group of top employees? If so, how? If not, can anything be done to increase their benefit without increasing the cost of benefits for all employees? For example, integrating the qualified retirement plans? (See Chapter 4 for an explanation of this important concept.)

☐ Who are the key employees? Why? Is their *position* key? Or are *they* the key?

☐ Am I interested in the possibility of key employees one day buying me out, in part or in whole? If so, do I have the type of key employees who are capable and motivated to one day run my company? Who are they?

☐ What promises have I made to key employees regarding (a) stock ownership, (b) participation in management, (c) sharing in profits of the company?

☐ Are existing employee incentive plans working?

☐ Are these plans consistent with my long-term retirement and financial goals? For example, if my key employees will not be buying me out, their incentives should be cash-based; if they are going to be the eventual owners, their benefits should be stock-based. In either case, is at least part of their incentive a golden handcuff that will provide motivation for them to remain with my company?

☐ Do I have in place sufficient protection should a key employee leave?

1. Covenant not to compete?
2. Covenant not to take other employees with him at employment?
3. Trade secrecy protection covenant?
4. Forfeiture provisions on deferred compensation or stock re-purchase agreements if covenants are violated?

☐ How are the incentive compensation packages reviewed, revised? How are their benefits effectively communicated to all concerned?

☐ Do the incentive packages appropriately reward the employee in terms of being

1. Financially attractive?
2. Founded on explicit performance standards?
3. Determinable in specific dollar amounts?
4. Awarded at least annually?
5. If no incentive package is now in place, how would I design one in terms of Questions 1 through 4?

☐ What detriments are there in implementing a plan in terms of cost and the possibility of upsetting nonparticipating good employees?

☐ Would money spent now on companywide benefits (e.g., a retirement plan) better serve my long-term goals by being reallocated to top employees?

☐ What is the best type of plan to motivate and retain my top employee(s)?

1. Cash-based or stock-based? Which is better?
2. If cash based:
   a. What amount?
   b. Based on what standards?
   c. When should I give it?
   d. How much should be deferred? Or subjected to golden handcuffs?
   c. What type of vesting schedule?

3. If stock-based, what terms and conditions should be placed on
   a. Stock bonus?
   b. Stock of cash bonus option?
   c. Stock option? If so, incentive stock option or nonqualified stock option?
   d. How is stock to be valued?
   e. How much stock is to be offered? Now and in the future?

4

A Dose of Castor Oil

What you need to know about taxes—no more, no less

As important as the subject is, there is no need for the business owner to be a *tax expert*. In fact, I can't think of any activity that will be less productive—and more taxing—than a self-imposed marathon over the labyrinthian course called the Internal Revenue Code. There are others you can hire who have that expertise. Your time should be spent on things you know best—and enjoy the most. After all, isn't that why you started your business?

Nevertheless, it's important that you have an understanding of the tax fundamentals that affect your business. You may find the subject a bit difficult, but try to stick with it; the knowledge you acquire will give you an edge that will equip you to ask the right questions of your advisors and comprehend their answers. You'll be able to make the kind of tax decisions that will help you achieve your planning goals and objectives. If you're already up to speed on the IRS Code, you may want to skip this chapter. You can always come back to it later.

To begin, let's recognize that there are two types of income tax problems: You've either paid too little and the IRS is now after you, or you've paid too much.

In the former case, there's not much you can do. The IRS is generally unyielding, and the enforcement laws favor them exclusively. Far more typical for the owners of closely held businesses is the situation where they've overpaid. Up to a point, it may be possible to recapture some of that overpayment. The only sure way to minimize your tax bite, however, is by thorough, thoughtful, and proper planning based on a conceptual framework of the basic tax issues facing business owners.

The framework concerns *rates, treatment,* and *timing.* These issues must be addressed and favorably resolved in the business setting in which they arise. For example, the questions of how your business is organized and what tax-favored employee benefit plans you will put into effect will be answered by resolving these issues.

Let's review each.

Tax Rates

You operate under one of four available options: a regular corporation (also called a C Corporation), a Subchapter S corporation (S Corporation) that has opted for special treatment under the Internal Revenue Code, a partnership, or a sole proprietorship. Depending on which form of business organization you've chosen, your tax rates (as well as tax treatment and tax timing) may be different.

Here's why:

A C Corporation has its own tax brackets that are different from those of its owners. For the first $50,000 of taxable income, the federal tax bite is 15 percent. The next bracket—$50,000 to $75,000—calls for a 25 percent rate. Above $75,000, the rate is 34 percent. Professional service corporations, such as those in the field of medicine, law, and accounting, pay a uniform 34 percent. The taxable incomes of all other types of business entities are taxed at the owners' income tax rate, generally an amount that does not exceed 28 percent.

As tax law changes, these rates change. At times the top bracket in a C Corporation is higher than an individual's top rate; at other times it's lower. The tax rate on a C Corporation's first bracket of taxable income has historically always been lower than an individual's top tax rate—usually at least 50 percent lower.

Another tax bracket differential can exist between individual taxpayers. For example, your tax rate on earned income might be significantly higher than your child's. *Wherever there is a difference in tax rates between business and an individual or between individuals, a tax planning opportunity exists* to shift the tax consequence to the taxpayer in the lowest tax bracket. The IRS is not unaware of this tax planning idea; but, surprisingly, the opportunity is ignored by many business owners.

For instance, most business owners understand the need to retain earnings at the business level to fund expansion, but they don't understand how they can take advantage of the tax system to reduce the overall cost of expansion. To grow, businesses need to add equipment, increase inventory, and hire more employees. Further, as accounts receivable grow in size, a timing difference is created between the increased production and the receipt of payment for that increased production; that is, in a growing business the billing increases while receipts lag.

Retained earnings provide the cash needed to fund these needs, but retained earnings are subject to income tax. Because a C Corporation has a lower initial tax bracket than does an individual (or S Corporation, partnership, or proprietorship), C Corporation status can be useful to entrepreneurial or growing businesses.

For example, if the corporate tax bracket is 15 percent, a business needs to earn a little less than $1.20 to end up with $1 after paying the tax ($1.20 × 85% = $1.02). On the other hand, if the marginal tax rate is 35 percent, a business needs to earn more than $1.50 in order to net $1 after taxes ($1.50 × 65% = $0.98).

If a business is not taxed at all on its retained earnings, obviously it need earn only $1 to retain $1. If the tax rate is 15 percent on the first $50,000 of retained taxable income, the total tax is $7,500, leaving $42,500 to be used by the business for its capital needs. If the tax rate is 35 percent, the total amount of taxes on the first $50,000 is $17,500, leaving $32,500 for the business.

Over time, that type of tax savings becomes significant because those savings can be reinvested by the business to provide many times the return.

Tax Treatment

When a business spends money, the result is one of three tax treatments:

1. The expenditure may be *nondeductible*, which means that it does not reduce the gross income of the business for tax purposes. This type of expenditure is often called after-tax spending. An example is the life insurance policy your company buys on your life because you are its "key" man or woman. Premium payments are nondeductible and consequently must be paid from income earned by the business after it has paid taxes on that income.

2. Money spent to buy a capital asset—machinery, office equipment, vehicles—is another expenditure. These assets can be *depreciated* over a number of years based on IRS guidelines on the useful life of the asset. A car or truck used in the business, for example, may be depreciated over not less than five years. If the vehicle cost $15,000, the payment of $15,000 would not be deductible in the year of purchase, but its depreciation is deductible. In this case the annual depreciation deduction is $3,000 (the $15,000 purchase price divided by the useful life of five years equals $3,000 per year depreci-

ation). At the end of the depreciation period, the business will have deducted the full purchase price of the equipment.

The depreciation schedules are based on the assumption that the equipment is useless at the end of the depreciation period and the company will need to repurchase new equipment. From a tax standpoint, it's clearly preferable to buy assets that can be depreciated over a period of time, rather than buying nondeductible assets.

3. Better yet is the tax treatment that permits a *total deduction*. The IRS allows businesses to deduct from their gross income all reasonable business expenses such as salaries, supplies and overhead expenses of rent, and short-term leases, among others.

Tax Timing

Deferring the incidence of taxation is critical. If you can delay the date the tax is imposed, you gain the use of the tax amount. There is great value—the *time value*—in this planning technique. For example, a 10 percent rate of return will cause an investment (in this case the amount of tax being deferred) to double every seven years. The greater the rate of return, the lesser the amount of time needed to double the investment. A sufficient deferral time and rate of return could mean the taxpayer could keep his cake (his money) and allow Uncle Sam to eat his too (the taxes).

In a real sense, tax timing is as good as avoiding a tax in the first place, since you are given opportunity to continue to use the taxed amounts. Thus a deferral of taxation is in a true sense tax avoidance.

As we shall see, deferral becomes an especially important planning concept in employee benefit planning—both yours and your employees. Further, the higher the current tax rate, the greater the benefit of deferring.

Let's look at how these three tax concepts can work together.

Assume that you have a C Corporation and at year-end have a net profit of $50,000. If you retain that profit in the corporation, it pays $7,500 in tax. If instead you pay yourself a bonus of that $50,000, the corporation then has no net profit because salaries are deductible. However, you have another $50,000 in taxable income and will pay approximately $15,000 in tax. On the other hand, if the corporation pays its net profit of $50,000 to its qualified retirement plan, it gets a deduction, has no taxable income left, and therefore pays no tax. Since you haven't received the income, you don't pay tax on it. Therefore you have deferred the income tax until you receive your retirement benefit. This is an example of the tax planning you can do.

Another example of the interrelationship of these tax concepts is the selection of the proper business entity form.

A "C" Corporation with its lower initial *tax rates* may be preferable to other types of business organizations if there will be an *ongoing need to accumulate capital* at the business level. The accumulation of capital always carries with it a *tax treatment* cost because it is nondeductible. Even where the capital accumulation will fund the purchase of depreciable equipment, the depreciation amount in the initial year will not be sufficient to pay for the tax cost of the initial accumulation.

On the other hand, where there is no need to accumulate capital, as may be the case with many service-oriented businesses, it's often preferable to avoid C Corporation status. The reason for this is that the distribution from the C Corporation to you is taxed to you. Unless that money can be taken out, such as in the form of a deductible expenditure to the corporation, usually a salary or bonus, this second tax will have to be paid without an offsetting deduction. This is a major consideration arguing against a C Corporation unless the need to accumulate capital is even stronger. Thus, to avoid the risk of a second tax being levied against corporate monies, an S Corporation is often appropriate.

On the basis of the relationship between the top bracket for individuals and the top bracket for corporations, it may also be appropriate to use an S corporation where large amounts of money—more than $100,000—must be retained by the company annually.

When this book was written, in 1989, the top individual bracket was six percentage points less than the top corporate bracket. Thus, for clients who needed to retain a large amount of taxable income at the business level, an S corporation was preferable. The monies retained would be taxed at the individual shareholder's bracket, and any advantage gained by an initial lower tax on the first $50,000 was overcome by the lower marginal rate on the much greater sum retained by the company. The form of organization selected for your business should be evaluated periodically in light of your business's capital accumulation needs and current tax law.

Employee Benefit Planning

In the broadest sense, employee benefits are those the company bestows upon one or more of its employees. Benefits are either "qualified" or "nonqualified." Let's look at the differences.

Qualified Benefits

"Qualified" employee benefits are those that are income tax deductible when paid by the business—benefits our good friends at the IRS have determined comply with the Internal Revenue Code.

A properly cynical business owner might ask, "Why would the IRS ever give a tax break to my business?" The answer is quite simple—to encourage businesses to provide the benefits Congress considers necessary for the public good but doesn't want to pay for. After all, if the private sector did not provide these benefits, the government might have to accept that responsibility.

To be ruled "qualified," the benefit must reach all or most of the employees in the company on a nondiscriminatory basis. This means the same type of benefit must be available to lower-paid as well as highly compensated employees.

Let's remember, though, that a primary objective of most business owners is often to gain as much of the tax-deductible employee benefit for themselves while minimizing the cost of providing benefits to their employees. This results in a constant tug-of-war between the government's desire to broaden the scope of qualified employee benefits to accomplish social goals and carry out tax policy on the one hand, and the goal of business owners to provide benefits to *selected* employees— themselves or key employees.

Qualified employee benefits focus on an employee's retirement, health, and disability. By extending tax benefits, Congress encourages businesses to provide these benefits to all its employees, including owners and other key employees.

The exact benefits available change almost yearly as Congress tinkers with the tax code, but generally they include group benefits, such as medical expense insurance, disability income, life insurance, dental insurance, and salary continuation plans, and cafeteria plans and other qualified retirement plans, including the 401(k) plan and defined benefit plan. Nonqualified benefits, such as deferred compensation plan, a split dollar insurance plan, a stock appreciation rights plan or phantom stock plan, and a stock bonus plan do not receive preferable income-tax treatment.

Employees preoccupied with medical problems cannot be productive employees. For that reason *medical expense insurance* for employees and their dependents is provided by enlightened business owners, along with a variety of other fringe benefits.

The IRS nudges business owners along this path by making the cost of providing this benefit a tax-deductible business expense while excluding those payments as taxable income to the employee. The coverage is available from many insurance firms, such as Blue Cross/Blue Shield, and an increasing number of health maintenance organizations (HMOs). Your financial planner or insurance agent will explain the range of coverage you can buy and the costs of such coverage.

Your advisor may also recommend that you provide some form of group *disability income* (sick pay or other short-term salary continuation benefit) to protect your employees against loss of income should they become disabled. Often this protection is provided directly by the employer with no insurance company involvement. However, long-term disabilities—two or three years or even a lifetime—will require you to look for coverage from an insurance company. Such coverage usually provides a percentage of income for a specified period of time.

As a corporation, you may also provide certain group *life insurance* to your employees and deduct the premium payments from your corporate taxes. The employee, too, is eligible for up to $50,000 of group term insurance paid by the employer without incurring imputed income from the premiums. If the insurance protection exceeds $50,000, the cost is includable in the employee's income according to his or her age and the amount of coverage.

In most circumstances, nondiscrimination rules practically eliminate the possibility of excluding any employees from participating in these group benefits.

Dental insurance is another discretionary benefit that has put the bite on business owners. Like corporate-provided medical expense insurance and disability insurance, coverage for dental care provides the same tax benefits in that premiums are tax-deductible for the employer for federal income tax purposes, but are not taxable income to the employee.

Salary continuation plans, because they are nonqualified plans, do not qualify for deductibility of funding contributions until the employee actually receives the benefit. These plans usually offer retirement benefits starting at age 65; they may continue for a specified number of years or as long as the retiree lives. Because no IRS approval is required and there are no nondiscrimination rules to comply with, these plans are favorably viewed by business owners for their flexibility. However, in part because the corporation does not get a taxable deduction for any prefunding of these plans, many plans remain unfunded and benefits are paid out of current operating funds.

Cafeteria plans provide employees a smorgasbord of non-taxable benefits from which to choose. Subject to nondiscrimination rules, a plan is considered discriminatory for any year in which the qualified benefits for key employees exceed 25 percent of such benefits provided for all employees. The penalties can be stiff. A well-paid employee will come face-to-face with a federal income tax liability on all qualified benefits provided on his behalf during the year.

Cafeteria plans provide employees with a choice of benefits—health insurance, reimbursement of medical expenses not covered by health insurance, disability insurance, or child care assistance. As the business owner, you can limit your cost by providing a fixed amount of money, say $100 per month. If health insurance premiums increase, the cost is passed on to the employee. If the employee wants additional benefits, he or she must pay for those extra benefits, but extra payments, if done via the cafeteria plan, are deductible by the employee.

This offers employees considerable flexibility in designing their own benefit package. It also allows your business to place a cap on the cost of the benefits you provide your employees. Suppose, for example, you decide to spend $100 per month for each employee. Your employee may take that money in cash (and pay the tax on it), or receive $100 worth of benefits under the cafeteria plan (all of which are tax-exempt to the employee).

Your financial planner will earn his fee by performing a detailed analysis to determine if a cafeteria plan makes sense for your business. Only the qualified employee retirement plans, however, offer owners a significant planning opportunity. We'll examine those shortly. But first let's look at an actual case history to see how retirement benefits can be used to an owner's advantage.

The Case of Dr. Felton

When I last met with Peter Felton, M.D., at his fiscal year-end meeting, we reviewed the status of his retirement plans with his accountant and financial planner. The retirement plans, established seven years previously, included a *money purchase plan* and a *profit-sharing plan.* How do they differ?

In the former the employer must put a stated percentage of his employee's pay into the plan annually. In the latter he has the annual option of putting anywhere from nothing to 15 percent of the employee's pay into the plan. Both plans are typically used in tandem in order to provide flexibility in contributions.

At the time the plans were established, Dr. Felton was making $150,000 a year and each of his two assistants was earning $15,000 annually. Contributions to the plan were income-tax-deductible to his business and were based on a percentage of each employee's compensation. Subject to "integration" (discussed later in this chapter), the contribution percentage amount had to be the same for each employee under the Internal Revenue Code.

The law also prevented the business from contributing more than $30,000 on behalf of a particular participant in any one year. That amount was also subject to a cap of 25 percent of that participant's compensation. In other words, if Dr. Felton had made only $100,000 in a particular year, the most that could have been put into the plan for his benefit was $25,000, or 25 percent of his total compensation. New employees could join the plan only after completing a full year with the business.

The last two planning variables we considered were the use of *integration* and the concept of *vesting.*

Integration incorporates the retirement benefit provided by Social Security in the formula used to determine contribution amounts to the plan's participants. The Social Security retirement benefit is based on the amount of income subject to the FICA tax each year.

In the year in question, the income amount subject to FICA—the "taxable wage base"—was about $48,000. Of the total Social Security contribution, the retirement percentage was approximately 5.7 percent. Therefore, for wages up to $48,000, the company was already paying 5.7 percent in retirement benefits. To keep things even, the IRS allows the business to put in an extra percentage (up to 5.7 percent) for compensation above the taxable wage base. The point where the employer kicks in the extra 5.7 percent is called the integration level.

Integrating the contributions with Social Security allows the employer to reduce the total plan cost while maximizing contribution levels for his key employees.

Let's review the following charts before we go into more detail:

	Dr. Felton	Employee A	Employee B
Compensation	$150,000	$15,000	$15,000
Money purchase contribution: 10%	15,000	1,500	1,500
5.7% on excess over $48,000	5,814	–0–	–0–
Total money purchase contributions	$ 20,814	$ 1,500	$ 1,500
Profit sharing: 6%	9,000	900	900
Total contributions both plans ($30,000 limit)	$ 29,814	$ 2,400	$ 2,400

Under the money purchase plan, we first allocated to all participants 10 percent of their compensation. For Dr. Felton this was $15,000. For each employee it was $1,500. An additional contribution of 5.7 percent was made for compensation above the integration level.

Notice that contributions above the integration level benefit only Dr. Felton. This is an integral part of the retirement planning for owners of closely held businesses. The total amount contributed under the money purchase plan was $23,814, *of which $20,814 is allocated exclusively to Dr. Felton.*

Since we are able to contribute a maximum of $30,000 on behalf of Dr. Felton, we also installed a profit sharing plan. Its sole purpose is to allow us to make additional contributions until his plan accounts total $30,000.

In our example we needed to contribute about 6 percent to Dr. Felton in order to have a total contribution of $30,000.

Of course, this means we contribute a like amount to each of the other participants since we can integrate only one plan.

At this point let's look at the advantages and disadvantages of the plan.

Advantages

The first advantage was that Dr. Felton was able to contribute $30,000 on a tax-deductible basis for his own retirement. As the trustee of the plan, he makes all investment decisions. (Giving this power to a doctor, however, can make even a cynical lawyer blanch!) As long as the contribution remains in the retirement plan, it earns money on a *tax-free* basis. When Dr. Felton eventually takes the money out of the plan for his retirement (after age 59½) he pays an income tax at the current tax rate. *The plan then has the best tax treatment and tax timing available. Money is deductible to the corporation going in, and all personal tax consequences to Dr. Felton are deferred until taken out.*

Also, depending on state law, the monies set aside in the retirement plan are not attachable by Dr. Felton's creditors, an important consideration for all professionals for whom liability or malpractice insurance may be too costly or impossible to obtain.

Another method to reduce overall employee costs is to subject the right to receive the monies set aside for an employee to "vesting." This means that unless an employee remains with the company for a specified number of years (generally, no more than six years), upon leaving the employee forfeits part of the monies set aside for his or her benefit.

Under Dr. Felton's plan, Employee A left after three years of participation and was entitled to only 40 percent of the account balance. The remaining 60 percent was used to reduce the contribution requirements of the company in the following year. In effect, the forfeited monies were reallocated to the accounts of Dr. Felton and Employee B, based on the ratio of their account balances. This meant that Dr. Felton received over 90 percent of the forfeited amount.

Of course, the biggest advantage is the income tax provision that allows the company to deduct money going in the plan and the owner/participant, Dr. Felton, to defer income tax consequences on that contributed amount and all its subsequent earnings until he takes it out. *This makes the qualified retirement plan the most significant form of tax deferral and tax avoidance device currently available to closely held businesses.*

A further advantage is the effect the retirement plan has on your employees. By subjecting their contributions to vesting, you can motivate them to remain with the company. I must say, however, that my experience with closely held businesses convinces me that employees—especially younger ones—rarely appreciate the amount of money allocated for their benefit until they quit and receive a tidy lump sum. Then they say, "Gosh, this is a lot of money. My employer really did a nice thing for me." By then, of course, it's too late, and the retirement plan has been ineffective in instilling a sense of loyalty.

Effective and continual communication of employee benefits, however, can heighten your employees' awareness of the value of their retirement plans. As they get older, their appreciation increases dramatically.

Finally, we shouldn't overlook the *primary advantage* of a retirement plan in your company: to provide *you* with a substantial retirement benefit. Without the tax advantages of the plan, it's often difficult for a business owner to save enough money outside of the business to provide for a comfortable retirement benefit.

Disadvantages

The first disadvantage of the plan is the cost of the contributions that must be made for the other employees. Aside from the integration amount, the percentage of contribution must be the same for them as it is for you. Generally speaking, you can only exclude employees from the plan who are under age

21 or who have been with the company for less than one year. In Dr. Felton's case, the employee cost was nominal—$4,500.

The reasonability of the employee cost is determined by looking at the amount of income tax Dr. Felton would have paid if he had taken the entire contribution amount, $34,500, as a bonus in the year of contribution assuming an effective personal tax bracket of 35 percent. The tax cost to Dr. Felton of taking the money now as compensation would be $12,075, a substantially more significant expense than the employee cost.

Obviously, as the number of your employee/participants increases, the percentage of the contribution your business makes to the plan on your behalf will decrease. At some level the employee cost may be too great, unless the benefit to the company as a tool for motivating and retaining good employees offsets the true cost of the plan.

In many of those situations, the most appropriate type of a retirement plan is the 401(k) plan, which is discussed later in this chapter.

A second disadvantage of retirement plans is the original cost to set them up, followed by the ongoing cost of maintaining and administering them. Plan administration can be complex and easily fouled up, and keeping plans current with the law can be overlooked by the business owner. That's why I recommend to my clients that they have three responsible individuals involved with their plan: an attorney, a financial planner, and an administrator.

Your *attorney* uses a prototype plan for you—one that has been preapproved by the IRS. As the law changes, the attorney makes those changes to his master plan and obtains approval from the IRS of those changes, which then will also apply to your plan with minimal further cost to you for amending the plan. (This cost saving is one reason I recommend attorney-based prototype plans as opposed to those available from an insurance company or bank. The latter usually want part of your investment business within the plan as the price of allowing you to use their prototype.)

The second individual on the team should be a good

financial planner who advises you on investments. It's helpful if the financial planner is also experienced in plan design and operation. His careful attention to your plan can be a safeguard against compliance or administrative errors.

The third person involved should be an *administrator*. In smaller plans this is often your own CPA. In large plans it's a "third party administrator" whose primary function is to administer retirement plans. This involves allocating the money to various plan accounts and preparing an informational return to the IRS on a periodic basis. The plan administrator also provides a statement each year to all employee/participants showing the amount of money in their account, the earnings achieved, and the current year's contribution from the employer to their account.

By having all three professionals work together, you assure that all three areas of plan compliance work and investments will be adequately covered. This discussion of Dr. Felton's plan has acquainted you with two different types of plans—the money purchase pension plan and the profit sharing plan. We've also reviewed such terms as vesting, integration, participation, nondiscrimination, and the tax benefits available with retirement plans.

Other types of qualified retirement plans may also be appropriate as your work force grows. Such plans include the 401 (k) plan and the defined benefit plan.

The *401 (k) plan* is a derivative of a profit sharing plan. It allows employees to contribute their own money to the plan on a tax-deferred basis. Often the employer agrees to match a certain percentage of the employee contribution. This employer match is the only cost to the employer of the plan other than the ongoing compliance costs.

Another type of retirement plan is known as a *defined benefit plan*. Unlike a defined contribution plan, which sets limits on the amount the employer can contribute to the plan on behalf of each employee, a defined benefit plan specifies the amount available to an employee upon his retirement. Annual contributions are then made so that the desired amount is available when the employee retires.

A defined benefit plan is now used only in special situations. Generally, to take advantage of the plan, the owner must be substantially older than his workers and willing to work ten years after the plan is established, usually until his retirement. In those special situations, however, it's possible to contribute considerably more than $30,000 a year on behalf of the employer/owner.

I've gone into a lot of detail on retirement plans simply because *they are the one remaining substantial tax benefit available to owners of closely held businesses.* Therefore, you need to understand how they work. You also need to know that as your business and employee work force expand, qualified retirement plans may make less sense. The employee cost may outweigh all other advantages. At that point, nonqualified deferred compensation may become more attractive.

Nonqualified Benefits

In contrast to the twin tax advantages of qualified plans, employer contributions to a nonqualified benefit plan are either deductible to the employer or not included in income by the employee, but not both. The primary attractiveness of a nonqualified plan is that it escapes the close scrutiny, supervision, and regulation of the IRS. As an owner you are able to determine which of your employees shall enjoy the benefits and how much each should get.

Indeed, this ability to single out an individual or small group of key employees and provide them benefits to the exclusion of all other employees, is the major reason to use nonqualified employee benefits. Since this type of plan requires either the business or the employee to bear some tax cost as funds are contributed to the plan, its usage must be carefully examined and its implications understood before it can be effectively employed.

A typical nonqualified plan may be a straightforward *deferred compensation plan,* a *split dollar insurance plan,* a *stock appreciation rights plan* or *phantom stock plan,* or a *stock bonus plan* (explained in detail in Chapter 3).

As with all tax-driven business decisions, nonqualified benefits should be considered in light of the conceptual framework of tax treatment, rate, and timing.

The tax code demands that the accumulation of funds for tax treatment, or simply for investment purposes, be a nondeductible event. Accordingly, the *tax rate* of the business becomes more important.

The law does not require a business to fund a nonqualified benefit as it does in the case of qualified plans. As a result there need not be a current cost or outlay of money by the business. In fact, major problems can arise if the business does fund the plan.

Nevertheless, the employees normally want some assurances that money will be there when they become entitled to benefits under the plan. Entitlement often occurs upon termination of employment because of retirement age, or because the employee or the business has achieved a certain long-term goal. Consequently, some method of "funding" usually is necessary; however, to avoid the pitfalls associated with the actual funding of a nonqualified plan, this "funding" is set up by the business with the understanding and agreement that the funds must be accessible to the business's general creditors. The business can take steps to further protect the benefit, such as agreeing not to use those funds or the earnings they generate as long as the business remains solvent, but the funds must always be available to the business's creditors.

To the extent there is funding, the tax rate *is* the business tax rate. For this reason you should consider the use of a C Corporation, because it has a low income tax bracket on the first $50,000 of taxable income. However, if this money is already being used for other nondeductible business purposes, then any further accumulation of taxable income would be taxed at the next corporate bracket, which may be higher than an individual's rates.

You can instantly see why a nonqualified plan can be either a benefit or a detriment to business owners. Why be taxed at a high corporate level when the monies can be currently distributed to you in the form of compensation and deducted by the business?

The tax bracket of the company should also be considered at that point when the benefits begin to be distributed out to the benefited employee. At that time the benefits are taxable to the employee as compensation and consequently deductible by the company as wages.

There is one aspect of a nonqualified plan which confers a *timing* benefit. This is the timing difference between the date the employee is given the benefit (with that money accruing at the corporate level) and the date he receives it. Often those funds are invested in an asset that accumulates income without current income taxation, such as a life insurance policy or annuity.

If the investment is in the form of a life insurance policy, the death proceeds are usually made payable to the corporation. At the employee's death, before or after he has received all of the deferred compensation, the death proceeds are generally received income tax free by the company. And when the company actually pays part or all of those proceeds as deferred compensation, it receives a deduction—proving that sometimes you do get something for nothing, or close to it.

Summary

I reiterate that there's no need for you to become a tax expert. You can always hire experts. In a sense, you need to know just enough tax theory to be slightly dangerous—to develop a sense of *when* to bring in expertise, and *why*. Remember that the mistakes owners of closely held businesses typically make involve overpayment of taxes, not underpayment. And overpayment is something that can often be avoided with a little help from an expert. Again, ask yourself the three questions to ensure you're on the right track:

1. If the transaction is nondeductible, is the taxpayer with the lowest tax *rate* paying for it?

2. What is the income tax *treatment* of the particular transaction?
3. What is the income tax *timing*?

You now know enough tax law to understand the tax fundamentals that affect your business. And you're dangerous!

Part II

Transferring Ownership and Value

Now that you're on the right track to creating and preserving value for your business interest, you need to know how to transfer it in exchange for money. For at some point you *will* be transferring your ownership interest. Hopefully, it will be under favorable and voluntary circumstances, such as a transfer during your lifetime to your son or daughter, a co-owner, a key employee, or a third party. But the transfer may also be triggered by an unfavorable and involuntary event, such as death or total disability.

In order for you and your family to obtain the maximum value of your ownership interest, it is vital that you begin planning now to cover both voluntary and involuntary transfers of that interest. I can't emphasize enough the critical difference a moderate amount of preplanning will make to you—both in terms of creating a market and value for your interest, and as a means of ensuring that you receive full payment for it.

5

Leaving Your Business Is Easier Than Leaving a Lover

The four basic ways—and how to pick the one that's best for you

After many years of building a thriving medical instruments business, Royce Cassidy, age 55, wanted to sell his business and retire to a leisurely life. But when he looked for possible buyers, he found no established market for his specialized business. And when he looked within his company, there was no one to buy it from him because—like most small business owners—he was the only one in the company who knew how to attract new business and run the operation. Only he possessed the entrepreneurial spirit and drive that had made his company successful.

Royce was looking straight into the mouth of an owner's worst retirement situation—liquidation.

As if starting and running a business isn't hard enough, there's the added difficulty of leaving a business you've created and nurtured. Usually the owner is too busy with the daily operations to think about it. And sometimes the prospect is such an emotional decision the owner doesn't want to think about it. In either case the vital task of planning for a smooth business succession is often postponed until the last minute.

Yet the best way to begin and operate a business is to realize that eventually you *will* leave it. And you will want to leave under terms that are most favorable to you. Retirement is the best way—your only alternatives being death, disability, and bankruptcy.

Bear in mind also that there are many reasons why an owner may *wish* to retire—some negative, some positive. They include advancing age, burnout, desire for a lifestyle change, boredom, need for a new challenge, disagreement with a partner, a family situation—the list is almost endless. Some days they seem to be happening simultaneously. But invariably at least one of these reasons exists.

One of the insights I've acquired over the years is that people get older. Everyone agrees that it makes sense to begin planning for retirement by building up savings and contributing to a retirement plan. Why not also plan to build up and cash in on your biggest investment—your business? It is also sound planning for your business to begin planning for your retirement. Take the case of Jim DeBoer, age 58.

Jim had started his manufacturing company over twenty-five years ago and took in Tom Metz as a partner ten years later, forming DMC Manufacturing Company. Now Jim and Tom own equal shares in the company. Jim wants to sell his shares to Tom and retire in a few years—if he can be guaranteed a good retirement income. To enable him to retain his lifestyle, Jim feels he'll need $500,000, but Tom, who is 41, doesn't have $25,000 in savings, let alone a half million.

That was their problem when they came to me. Before I explain the plan I came up with to resolve their dilemma, it's important to lay some groundwork that applies to your business as well.

Remember a few years back when Paul Simon's hit song told us there were "fifty ways to leave your lover"? Well, here's good news: Basically, there are only four ways to leave your business. If you know these methods and decide in advance which one you prefer, then you can look forward to leaving your business under terms and conditions you choose. Without planning you are more likely to settle for terms and conditions beyond your control.

Here, listed in the most desirable order, are the four most common ways you can leave your business:

1. Transfer ownership to your kids or other family members.
2. Sell your interest to co-owners, key employees, or all your employees.
3. Sell to a third party such as a competitor or someone interested in entering your business.
4. Liquidate by selling off your assets, usually at "fire sale" prices.

Because your business is so personal to you, turning it over to your children, or to those who helped you succeed, is a more satisfying prospect than putting it in the hands of some stranger—although, I suppose, that really depends on your kids (see Chapter 8). And obviously, liquidation, the last of these choices, should be avoided, since liquidation is not really a choice but a last-resort action that offers the least reward in terms of cash. It also terminates your business as an ongoing enterprise. (And there goes your last chance for immortality!)

There are pluses and minuses in each method. Knowing what they are will help you determine which method is most suitable for you. It will be useful to summarize the characteristics of each method so that you can compare the relative merits and disadvantages before making your decision.

In comparing each method, we need to look at six common elements: (1) minimizing risk, (2) exercising control, (3) achieving personal and nonbusiness objectives, (4) assuring payment, (5) maximizing flexibility in structuring the deal, and (6) fixing value. These elements apply in varying degrees to each method of sale.

Now let's look at the four methods.

Transfer of Ownership to Your Children

On the downside is the possibility that this transaction simply won't work. In other words you won't get paid off, there will be friction and increased family tension, nonfamily key employees will resent working for Junior, and you will wind up having to go back to work. Nonbusiness factors and personal objectives always enter into a transaction involving your children, significantly increasing the risk. And because of family ties, you can suffer loss of control even without losing voting control.

On the other hand, this method offers you unequaled opportunity to exercise control and write your own departure ticket in terms of how much money you will get and when you will get it. Moreover, transferring ownership to your children enables you to fix value by starting with the question *"How much do I need or want?"* rather than being told, *"This is how much I am willing to give you."* And certainly there are few areas in life where more satisfaction can be gained than to see your business successfully continued by your offspring.

Because this is one of the most desirable and most frequently used ways to leave a business, as well as the most risky, the subject is reviewed in depth in Chapter 8. I think you'll find it interesting reading even if you won't be transferring your business to your children—provided, of course, you like TV family gut wrenchers like "Dallas," "Dynasty," and "Falcon Crest."

Sale to Other Owners, Employees, or Shareholders

One of the great advantages of having other owners in your business is that they can be your means to retirement. In fact, a common retirement planning technique is to have a younger individual buy into your business while you are still active. Upon your retirement, the younger shareholder will purchase your remaining stock.

This can be advantageous because the younger person will learn the business—its structure, employees, customers, operation, and management. More important for you, the younger person's capabilities (as well as his weaknesses) are known to you, so you have a pretty good idea how your business will be run after you leave. And most important of all, the business can be sold to a market you create and control.

This latter feature provides you with an unsurpassed opportunity to

- Structure the deal ahead of time.
- Create value.
- Establish a fund inside the business for the purchase of your interest.
- Maintain a greater measure of control after the buyout.
- Prequalify the buyer(s) through on-the-job training and observation.

A side benefit of planning a buyout is that the steps you take to build value and train future new owners also will make the business more profitable, more stable, and better-managed—even if you decide to postpone your retirement.

Thus, grooming the "heir apparent" allows you to slow down, to have an option on your future that will give you flexibility in case the unexpected happens, such as becoming suddenly disabled or inheriting a bundle from Aunt Emma. At the same time you've developed a stronger business, both from a financial as well as an employee standpoint.

To summarize in terms of the six common elements:

1. *Risk* is minimized because dealings with co-owners or employees are usually at arms length and the personal factors that increase risk may not be present as they are when you

transfer your interest to family members. Also, since you handpicked your employees or co-owners, you should know if the company will continue to prosper after your retirement.

2. *Control* of the business can be maintained through the initial phases of the buyout, which usually begins while you are still active and the initial stock purchase is of a noncontrolling portion—often 10 to 30 percent. Voting control does not need to pass until 50 percent of the stock is paid for. Thereafter, payment for the remaining 50 percent of the ownership interest can be secured by the assets of the business. This reduces the risk that the sale will turn sour during the early phases of the buyout. After voting control has passed, control can be indirectly maintained through provisions in the purchase agreement dealing with collateral, security, and performance guarantees. (The particulars of this arrangement are discussed in detail in Chapter 6.)

3. *Personal or nonbusiness objectives* are normally not a paramount consideration when you sell to anyone other than your own family members. However, many owners want to see their "baby" continue to grow, their key employees and co-owners rewarded, and the rest of their employees assured job security. These objectives can best be achieved by selling out to existing key employees or co-owners rather than to a third party.

4. *Payment* is best assured through prefunding and a careful transition plan calling for your gradual retirement and periodic sale of stock to avoid a business or marketing disruption.

5. *Flexibility* in structuring the deal is maximized by the very process of putting a successor in place before the buyout occurs. This gives you the luxury of time to undo a poor selection or to speed up your retirement, if a capable successor is found and greener pastures await you. Finally, because control is maintained until the buyout is substantially completed, the deal can be changed to meet unforeseen conditions that always seem to crop up.

6. *Determining value* usually is not adversarial. After all,

the new owners have helped create the value and therefore will more likely recognize nontangible valuation factors. Also, you control the value determination process to a significant degree because of your overall control of the company. Your purchasers need to know, early on, the formula for valuation. Their consensus must be obtained. Determining value, then, is often a matter of your coming up with a fair selling price, getting the buyers to agree to its fairness, and implementing a payment plan.

Sale to a Third Party

In a retirement situation, sale to a third party too often becomes a bargain sale—the only alternative to liquidation. This option becomes necessary because you have failed to create a market for your stock through sale to your family, co-owners, or employees. The problems—and opportunities—inherent in this situation are reviewed in greater detail in Chapter 7, but a few observations are in order at this time.

If you decide to sell to an outside party, here are some of the things you must contend with:

- An outside party will have more bargaining power and, consequently, the ability to drive a hard bargain.
- An outside owner is an unknown quantity in terms of his management style and his "fit" with other employees and your customers.
- Some, or most, of the purchase price will likely have to be carried so the new owner's competence, which is unknown, becomes a critical factor.
- You will probably be required to remain with the company for one to three years under the terms of the purchase agreement. This allows for business transition to the new ownership. I have yet to find an entrepreneur who relishes working for someone else at his or her former business. This is a most difficult time for former owners. They would really prefer being somewhere

else—at a golf resort, for example, enjoying their retirement.

Of course, there are several advantages of a third-party
sale. Often it can be the best way to maximize value at your
retirement as well as assuring that your employees will continue to have jobs. Sometimes, selling to a third party is more
beneficial or practical than selling to other owners or employees. This is particularly true in a business too small to support
other owners or key employees, or in a large business where
the value exceeds the amount the owners and/or key employees realistically can pay. The planning techniques in selling a
business to a third party are discussed in Chapter 7.

Looking at this method from the standpoint of the six
common elements, we can make these conclusions:

- *Risk:* Since you're probably dealing with an unknown
  party, you'll want the largest possible down payment to
  minimize your risk.
- *Control:* Selling to a third party usually means unload-
  ing all of your interest at once. Therefore, the only
  control you'll retain is that provided in a thorough and
  properly drafted purchase agreement, including adequate collateral and security arrangements.
- *Personal objectives:* Other than cashing out, a sale to a
  third party usually accomplishes little in the way of
  secondary objectives. You do not know how a new
  owner is going to treat your customers or your employees, or what will happen to the reputation of your
  business. As for nonbusiness factors, there are none.
- *Assurance of payment:* Because there are so many un-
  knowns, you must receive at least 25 to 60 percent of
  the purchase price up front. The balance must be fully
  collateralized and secured, with both the business assets and the buyer's personal assets, as well as the
  personal guarantee of the purchaser.
- *Flexibility in structuring the deal:* This depends on the
  strength of your bargaining position. Here's where the

negotiating skills of your advisors—your lawyer and accountant—are critical. If you need to retire quickly, your bargaining position may be weak and your ability to design the buyout hampered.

- *Value:* Fair market value has been defined as "the price that a willing purchaser would pay for assets being sold by a willing seller." This scenario works when you are selling a can of soup, but it doesn't work as well when you are selling a closely held business. Timing is critical because value can be greatly affected if bargaining is influenced by economic, political, and governmental factors beyond your control.

Liquidation

If there is no one to buy your business, you shut it down. In a liquidation the owners sell off their assets, collect outstanding accounts receivable, pay off their bills, and keep what's left, if anything, for themselves.

Because the business does not continue and the assets normally are sold for cash, factors such as risk, control, payment, and attainment of personal objectives simply do not exist. There is no deal to be structured. The chief concerns often are being certain to be able to obtain fair value for the assets, pay off all liabilities, and then deal with income tax consequences. Careful preplanning can minimize the tax impact, but can do little to create value.

Service businesses in particular are thought to have little value when the owner leaves the business. This certainly is true if liquidation occurs.

Since most service businesses have little "hard value" other than accounts receivable, this means of retirement produces the smallest return for the owner's lifelong commitment to his business. *In a service business with little accumulated assets, liquidation is preferable only to death as a means of getting money out of your business.* Smart owners guard against this. They plan ahead to ensure that they do not have to rely on this means to retire.

Up to this point we've looked briefly at the four ways to leave your business. Other than the liquidation method, each method contains not only related characteristics, but also substantial and often dramatic differences. These are reviewed in greater detail in the following chapters. Chapter 6 analyzes the sale of your business interest to co-owners or key employees. Chapter 7 reviews the sale to a third party. Also, in Chapter 8, you'll get a closer look at the method of transferring ownership to your children.

You now know the four basic ways to leave your business, and the general characteristics of each. Put this knowledge to good use by answering the questions listed in the checklist that follows. This exercise will help you determine which qualities appeal to you most and which least fit your business. Remember the six factors to be considered: (1) minimizing risk, (2) exercising control, (3) achieving personal and non-business objectives, (4) assuring payment, (5) maximizing flexibility in structuring the deal, and (6) fixing value.

FOUR WAYS TO LEAVE YOUR BUSINESS CHECKLIST

☐ 1. Transfer of business to children:

    a. This method appeals to me because: _____

    _____

    b. This method might be appropriate for my business for the

    following reasons: _____

    _____

    c. This method would be appropriate only if the following

    conditions were present: _____

    _____

    d. This method is inappropriate for me and my business for

    these reasons: _____

_____

☐ 2. Sale to co-owners, key employees, or all employees:

    a. This method appeals to me because: _____

_____

    b. This method might be appropriate for my business for the

    following reasons: _____

_____

    c. This method would be appropriate for my business only if

    the following conditions were present: _____

_____

    d. This method is inappropriate for me and my business for

    these reasons: _____

_____

☐ 3. Sale to a third party:

    a. This method appeals to me because: _____

_____

    b. This method might be appropriate for my business for the

    following reasons: _____

_____

    c. This method would be appropriate for my business only if

    the following conditions were present: _____

_____

    d. This method is inappropriate for me and my business for

       these reasons: _____

_____

☐ 4. Liquidation: This should be used only as a last resort. Don't
even consider this.

Once you have completed the previous exercise, ask yourself the following questions:

- What is my targeted retirement date? (Pick a month and
a year.)

_____

- How much money do I want to have in my personal
savings when I retire? _____
- How much money will I need each year to retire comfortably?

_____

(Disregard the effects of inflation for now.)
- Do my current advisors (legal, accounting, business
consultant, financial planner, and others) have the experience to help me plan the transition of my business?
Are they creative, good listeners, insightful? Can they
benefit me because they've done it all many times before? _____

_____

6

A Gold Watch and a Kiss on the Forehead

Selling your business to co-owners or employees

You've been thinking about it all year. This morning you woke up and, over a cup of coffee, told your spouse, *"I've made up my mind. I'm going to sell out. Then we're going to take that long, long vacation we've always talked about."*

But how do you proceed?

First, revive your spouse. Then look at the best way to structure a retirement buyout by asking yourself these fundamental questions:

1. What are the income tax consequences of the transaction?
2. What are you selling?
3. Who is the purchaser?

The first question is a big one and must be carefully considered, preferably long before the owner retires, to maximize retirement income. But, in answering the tax question, other questions must be addressed.

One way of approaching income tax analysis is to look at

what you are selling. Is it services rendered or to be rendered, or is it an asset or product? How this question is answered can make a huge difference in the amount of money you will receive. *By planning ahead, you can determine the answer in advance.*

When an owner retires and sells his stock to another shareholder, he is obviously selling an asset or product, the ownership interest in the business. But viewed differently, what the owner is giving up is an income stream—his salary, bonus, and other benefits that he had previously enjoyed while he was the owner of the company. In selling his stock, he is trying to replace that income stream.

Under the 1986 Tax Reform Act, the difference in income rates between capital gain income (income from the sale of capital assets) and income from wages is eliminated. The top bracket for both types of income is 28 percent. The elimination of the difference in rates must be considered in designing how the business or the remaining shareholders are going to acquire the owner's interests.

Incorporating that understanding into retirement planning may mean as much as 25 percent *more money, after tax.* Looked at another way, it may mean the owner can retire 25 percent earlier than otherwise planned.

The tax question may be answered differently depending on *whom* you sell to. One potential purchaser of your stock is your employees—possibly through an Employee Stock Ownership Plan (ESOP). You may be able to defer—even eliminate—all taxes on the proceeds you'll get from such a stock sale.

Thus, as the owner, you must ask yourself, In what form do I want to receive my retirement monies? There are four primary ways to do this. Let's look at each.

Sale of Stock to Shareholders or Key Employees

If the retirement monies are in the form of the sale of their business, the owners who are retiring will pay a federal tax, currently at 28 percent, on the difference between the price received for their stock and their *basis* in the stock. In selling your business interest to an insider, you will normally be selling stock as opposed to the assets of the business. Without getting too technical, *basis* is ordinarily the price the owner originally paid for the stock. Basis can also be affected by distributions made in respect to that stock, especially in S Corporations.

In most closely held businesses, the owner's basis is very low in comparison to the ultimate selling price. In that case most of the purchase price paid will be subject to taxes at 28 percent. If you, the owner, are to receive $1 million for your business interest, and we assume your basis is zero, you will be taxed on the entire $1 million gain received.

The real question is *To what extent* will the total monies you receive be from stock sale proceeds, and how much will be by alternative methods? The alternative methods transfer money—but not for stock itself—from the purchaser to you. Accordingly, they are used in conjunction with a sale of stock because they may offer tax advantages.

Use of Deferred Compensation

If you had continued to receive compensation from the business totaling $1 million after retirement, the tax consequences would be the same—that is, a tax, currently at the rate of 28 percent, would be imposed on the money received. Thus, there is no difference from a tax standpoint to you between the sale of your stock and receipt of earned income, other than the reduction in the gain from the sale of stock due to your cost basis.

On the other hand, there is a dramatic difference in tax impact at the corporate level. If the corporation is in a 34 percent tax bracket and is paying $1 million for the purchase of the stock, it will have to earn $1.5 million and pay a maximum tax of 34 percent to leave a net of $1 million available for the purchase of the stock.

Accountants and tax lawyers—with our flair for words—call the purchase of a stock by a corporation an "after tax event"—meaning it is nondeductible. If, however, the corporation continues to pay the owner compensation at the rate of $100,000 a year for ten years, it need earn only $1 million, since the payment of compensation is a deductible event for the corporation.

This method results in a substantial cash-flow difference to the corporation—50 percent—but of little or no consequence to the departing owner, as can be seen in the next method.

Using Increased Retirement Funding

You should already be aware of the tax advantages of retirement plans. If not, take a deep breath and reread the information on tax (or is it taxing?) in Chapter 4. Contributions to such a plan by the business are deductible, and the tax on income earned through the plan for your benefit is deferred until you withdraw the money from the plan. Ordinarily these plans cannot discriminate in your favor as the owner; any funding for your benefit would also have to benefit the other participating employees.

But through proper design of the plan, you can increase the amount of your benefit relative to the other co-owners or key employees who are also purchasing the stock. This will change the character—and therefore the tax treatment of payments to you, the retiring owner—but not the total amount of your payment.

In companies where you and the purchasers of your stock are the only significant participants in the retirement plan, it may be possible to have them (if they are highly compensated individuals) opt out of the retirement plan. At the same time, the funding formula can be increased so that a greater amount of retirement plan benefits accumulate for you, but not the other, and presumably younger, participants. You will then receive a disproportionate amount of the company's cash flow as a retirement plan contribution.

In order to pay the increased funding requirement of the plan for your benefit, the other co-owners or key employees may even reduce their current salary. Thus, if there is enough time, the company can begin paying you more current salary as well as more contributions made solely on your behalf into the retirement plans. The sum of these monies will reduce the amount of money you will need to have paid to you by other means at your actual retirement.

Using an ESOP

Recently one of our clients sold his stock in his closely held business. The transaction benefited him, the business, and the employees. Our client realized no taxable gain, the company earned a tax break, and the employees received a benefit plan that eventually will make them their own employers. Something straight from Aesop's Fables? Well, sort of. It was an ESOP.

The ESOP is more than just another qualified retirement plan recognized by the Internal Revenue Code. When considering the 1986 Tax Reform Act, the U.S. Senate recognized ESOPs as "a bold and innovative technique for strengthening the free private enterprise system." As a result of this strong congressional support, ESOPs came through the tax reform process relatively unscathed. In fact, some commentators believe that ESOPs are more attractive than ever.

So just what is an ESOP?

It's a qualified plan, usually profit-sharing, adopted by an employer corporation which is designed to invest primarily in the employer's stock. There are many ways for the ESOP to acquire and finance that stock, each a method having different business and tax advantages. For example, the client described above sold his stock directly to the ESOP in order to achieve the results I mentioned.

The stock contained in the ESOP, or its value in cash, is

distributed to participants of the ESOP upon their termination of employment. As in other qualified plans, certain participation and vesting requirements will limit the available benefits.

In a closely held business, the ESOP provides a buyer for the owner's stock, *a buyer who might otherwise not exist.* ESOPs can also be pivotal in the structure of a leveraged buyout of a company by co-owners, employees, or third parties.

The most touted ESOP incentive allows you to sell your stock to an ESOP and to *defer all gain* on that sale if you reinvest the proceeds in the stock of other operating companies, such as General Motors.

To make it easier for ESOPs to purchase stock, the tax law allows a bank making a stock purchase loan to an ESOP to report as income only half of the interest it received. Thus, ESOPs can secure below-market-rate loans.

So much for laying the groundwork. As we've seen, a stock purchase is generally nondeductible to the buyer. The payment for the stock is ordinarily completely taxable to you after you have recovered your cost basis. Deferred compensation is fully deductible by the business and fully taxable to you. Retirement plan funding is fully deductible by the business and tax-deferred to you. Sale of stock via an ESOP results in deductibility by the corporation and long-term, perhaps permanent, tax deferral to you and your family.

Thus, there is a sliding scale of income tax benefits. But like everything else in business, there is no free lunch—any tax-advantaged transaction carries with it certain obligations and increased complexity that may cause you to prefer a simple stock sale.

Now, let's get back to our case history.

Remember Jim DeBoer and his junior partner, Tom Metz? If you recall, Jim wanted to retire with a half-million bucks, but his partner couldn't come close to buying him out. Tom knew that if DeBoer-Metz Corporation would purchase Jim's stock, Tom would own 100 percent of the outstanding stock. And there was cash flow at the corporate level to pay Jim $500,000—if it could be spread over a ten-year period. But there were complications.

If the company purchased Jim's stock for $500,000 payable over ten years, it would need to pay about $40,000 in interest annually during the initial years, plus an annual $50,000 principal payment. As a nondeductible item, the principal payment would require the company to use taxable income of $75,000 and pay taxes of about $25,000 on that $75,000 to have $50,000 left over.

In addition to the $75,000, the company would also have to pay interest of $40,000 and would use another $50,000, pretax, in order to fund the ongoing capital needs of the business, such as equipment replacements, leasehold improvements, and other items. Therefore, the business would need to earn, *before tax,* $165,000.

Since Jim's salary had been $75,000 a year, including bonus, and the company systematically retained $50,000 for capital needs, there would be a shortfall of about $40,000 during the initial years, decreasing to less than $20,000 as the principal was paid down in later years. A cash flow shortfall like this is typical in "boot strap" acquisitions or leveraged buyout situations.

What to do? We looked at three possibilities in conjunction with a stock sale:

1. A retirement plan.
2. Deferred compensation plus an ESOP plan.
3. Deferred compensation without an ESOP plan.

First, we looked at using the company's existing retirement plan in terms of increasing the company's contributions to De-Boer while decreasing Metz's salary. The company had been contributing about $20,000 a year to the company's retirement plan. By changing the type of retirement plan from a profit-sharing plan to a defined benefit plan, decreasing Metz's salary slightly to partly allow for the increased amount of contributions, and having Metz elect not to participate in the new plan, the proposed total of compensation plus retirement plan contributions for each owner looked like this:

Metz: $60,000, all compensation.
DeBoer: $75,000 compensation, plus $75,000 plan contribution.

Since we integrated the defined benefit plan (see explanation of "integration" in Chapter 4), and the other employees were all fairly young, only a small portion of the defined benefit annual contribution—about $10,000—was allocated to them.

Unfortunately, we didn't have the luxury of time. This type of retirement plan funding needs time while DeBoer is still an employee of the company. If we had three years, we probably could have funded about $300,000 for DeBoer. Combined with a stock sale for $200,000, he would have had his half million. But he wanted to retire much sooner than that.

Nevertheless, this example illustrates the important point that there is still a considerable amount of flexibility in designing retirement plans to benefit primarily the departing shareholder under the following circumstances:

- He is from fifty to sixty years old.
- The other co-owners are highly compensated and therefore can elect not to participate.
- There is enough time, five years or so, to fund the plan.
- The other employees who participate in the plan do not take a large proportion of the plan contribution, because they are few in number and, for the most part, considerably younger than the departing owner.
- The co-owners can reduce their current compensation enough to make cash available to meet the company's increased contribution requirement.

Next, we looked at using an ESOP as a method of getting money to DeBoer. Under this method, DeBoer would sell his stock valued at $300,000—an amount an appraiser thought equal to fair market value—to the ESOP. DeBoer would receive deferred compensation payments totaling $200,000 from the business.

DeBoer would pay no taxes on the $300,000 received from ESOP if he reinvested the proceeds in qualifying securities—essentially stock and securities in companies that operate ongoing businesses. He would pay taxes on the $300,000 when he sells the qualifying securities. He would have to pay income taxes on the deferred compensation as he received it.

The ESOP would obtain the $300,000 cash by borrowing from a bank at a reduced loan rate. Banks are generally eager to make

ESOP loans because they need only to take into account one half of the interest income earned on the loan in their own income tax. The loan would be secured by the assets of the DeBoer/Metz Corporation, personally guaranteed by Metz, and paid off by annual contributions to the ESOP from the business over a seven-year period.

There are substantial advantages in using an ESOP for the selling shareholder. He gets a significant amount, if not all, of his selling price up front; and there is a potential deferral of the gain until he ultimately sells the reinvested securities. If he holds the securities until death, his estate can even avoid paying income taxes on the gain.

The remaining shareholders stand to benefit as well. The payoff of $300,000 to DeBoer is, in effect, tax-deductible by the company, since it pays the debt off through its tax-deductible contributions to the ESOP plan. Meanwhile, Metz remains firmly in control of the company since he already owns half of it and will elect himself as trustee of the ESOP plan. Although the participants within the plan are entitled to vote on significant corporate decisions, the day-to-day operation of the company will be made by Metz.

The primary disadvantage to Metz, however, is that he would own not 100 percent of the stock when an ESOP is involved, but only 50 percent. Only half of any future appreciation in value of the company would benefit him. Metz could increase his ownership interest by agreeing, or having the corporation agree, to buy some of DeBoer's stock instead of the ESOP buying all of it.

An additional disadvantage was that as the participants of the ESOP plan leave the company through retirement and request their retirement plan share, the company will need to redeem the stock otherwise owned by the departing employees. That redemption is not tax-deductible and, in a sense, is paying for the stock for a second time—once through the original retirement plan contribution and a second time when the stock is redeemed.

For these reasons DMC decided not to install an ESOP plan. (However, another owner may have found it ideal, especially if that owner wanted a large sum of money up front and the other co-owner or key employees were not in as significant a bargaining position as was Metz.)

In addition to a stock purchase, we finally settled on our third option: deferred compensation. Here's why:

Instead of having the company pay $500,000 for Jim's stock, the accountants assured us that they could justify a value of $200,000 for his stock as its fair market value. The remaining $300,000 could be paid to Jim in the form of deferred compensation.

Since Jim's *basis* in the stock was only $25,000, his tax consequences would be exactly the same—that is, he would have experienced a recovery of basis of $25,000 and all the remaining payments from the corporation, under either scenario, would be taxed at the same income tax rate.

The corporation's initial cash flow needs under each scenario can be seen in Charts I and II:

Chart I. Stock sale only.

	Cash Needed Annually After Tax	Cash Needed Annually Before Tax
Installment payments:		
Principal	$50,000	$ 75,000
Interest	40,000	40,000
Deferred compensation	0	0
Total	$90,000	$115,000

Chart II. Stock sale and deferred compensation.

	Cash Needed Annually After Tax	Cash Needed Annually Before Tax
Installment payments:		
Principal	$20,000	$25,000
Interest	16,000	16,000
Deferred compensation	50,000	50,000
Total	$86,000	$91,000

The advantages of proper tax planning should be apparent in the above example. As can be seen, DeBoer receives roughly the same amount under either scenario. The corporation, however, saves $150,000 (about a third of the total cost) over a ten-year period through such planning, because the funds are not going to Uncle Sam. These additional monies can be kept either at the corporate level, distributed to the departing shareholder, or divided in some proportion between the corporation and the departing owner.

At first glance it would seem that the departing shareholder would always want the entire savings passed on to him. However, in any type of installment buyout, the individual who is leaving the company must be concerned with its future economic health and profitability—if he expects to receive his payout over time. Therefore, easing the tax burden to the company is one way to help ensure future payments. In our example the extra money was needed at the business level to make the deal work.

The lesson to be learned here is that because of substantial tax advantages to the corporation and the lack of any offsetting tax disadvantage to the departing shareholder, deferred compensation is a vital element in tax planning, especially planning for retirement. It's important to install a deferred compensation agreement long before your actual retirement so that the IRS has no justification to tie the agreement to the sale of your stock. Otherwise the IRS might argue that the deferred compensation is payment for the sale of stock.

And how about Royce Cassidy, whom we met in Chapter 3? He told me his company had earned $450,000 in taxable income the previous year, but the strain of running the business virtually single-handedly was too much to continue. In seeking a buyer, he discovered to his surprise that he himself was the company's most valuable asset. Without his presence to oversee day-to-day operations, no one was interested in buying him out.

He soon realized his best alternative was to remain on the job while he found, trained, and delegated responsibilities to key employees who could replace his technical and marketing skills. After twice picking the wrong person, he finally found two people he had confidence in. One was a skilled marketer; the other possessed a background in operations. Cassidy provided them with an incentive and ownership package that motivated them to stay with the company. He also gave his business added protection by insisting they agree to trade secret and noncompete provisions in their employment agreements.

A deferred compensation agreement was implemented and partial funding was accomplished by keeping the salaries of the two key employees lower than they otherwise would have been. This again gave the key employees a stake in the future. They would want to be around when Cassidy did leave, since they paid—indirectly—for the deferred compensation. It also gave Cassidy and the employees more assurance that the payment could be made upon his retirement.

The two key employees eventually will own the business, which is worth much more than they could ever hope to purchase with their own funds. At the same time, Cassidy will hop along into a comfortable retirement, albeit years later than he wished to, but confident that he has the right personnel in position to replace him and some of the funding already done. Should one or the other falter, Cassidy has retained the ability to replace them through buy-back agreements.

Cassidy eventually found a solution. It's too bad, though, that he took so long to recognize his problem. Ideally, his search for replacement ownership should have begun much earlier—soon after he started his company. That way the business would have had more time to test and build a management team, more time to make—and learn from—mistakes.

Summary

The central message of this chapter is simply this: In addition to death and taxes, there is the certainty that sooner or later you will depart from your business. How handsomely you reward yourself on that occasion depends on the retirement plan you put into motion today. The more time you give yourself, the greater range of options you will have.

We've explored several ways to transfer ownership to your employees or co-owners. The particular method, or methods, you select depends on several factors. The first factor is *time:* When do you want to retire? Set a date now. At that time, do you want to retire *completely* or work on a *reduced schedule?*

If your retirement date is less than five years away, you probably haven't enough time to fund a defined benefit retirement plan or even to properly establish and fund a deferred compensation program. A leveraged ESOP buyout can work as well as a straightforward stock sale. However, you may want to give yourself more time than three years, even with a stock sale or an ESOP buyout. If you can allow five years before you retire, then any method, and any combination of methods, can usually be made to work. Consider what's just been discussed by answering the questions in the following checklist.

TRANSFER OF OWNERSHIP CHECKLIST

☐ Whom do you wish to sell to?

☐ Do the potential buyer, or buyers, have as much skill as you do?

☐ With your retirement, what gaps in the running of the business need to be filled?

☐ Will the new owner(s) have the skills to fill those gaps?

☐ If not, what is the best way of finding someone who has the required skills?

☐ When should the new owner(s) be brought on board?

☐ Will they need to own stock as well?

☐ How much is your business worth today?

☐ How much will the business likely be worth at your planned retirement date?

☐ How much money do you need from the business in total? And what form can this payment take? For example, lump sum? Per year? For how many years?

☐ How much money do you need to live on after retirement? What portion of that amount must come from the proceeds of the sale of your business?

These are all simple questions. They are questions most people never ask themselves. Yet, if you have no goal or objectives to reach for, how can you attain a satisfactory retirement? Set these goals now and review them periodically. Revise as needed.

The answers to these questions may also help determine the form the buyout must take. For example, if you feel the need for a large amount of cash up front, deferred compensation is not the answer; perhaps a stock sale or an ESOP, either one financed with a bank loan, would be more appropriate.

7

From Swampland to Alligator Farm

Selling to a third party—why, when, and how

Other than liquidating your business, selling it to a stranger—or at least to a third party—is often a last resort. But it can be a very nice last resort. In fact, you may end up at the resort of your choice.

In my experience, most owners end up transferring their business to co-owners, employees, or their family. You can control the conditions and terms of the transfer of your stock to these groups much more than in a sale to third parties. Nevertheless, there are three basic situations where a third-party sale is preferable to any other:

1. The business is too valuable to be purchased by anyone other than someone who has access to a considerable source of money.
2. There is no prospective buyer among your children or employees who desires to, and is capable of, running the business.
3. You want to receive a substantial amount of cash at the

closing, an unlikely event if you sell to a co-owner, an employee, or a family member.

Usually, a third-party sale results from a combination of these factors.

Of course, it is of the utmost importance that you assemble a strong management team that could someday assume ownership. In some smaller businesses that can't support a management infrastructure, that's just not feasible. But even if it is, you might choose to at least consider the third-party alternative for several reasons:

- You want to receive most of your selling price up front.
- An additional cash infusion into the business is needed for it to remain viable after your departure.
- Your employees or co-owners are willing to purchase only *part* of your business.

Should any of these conditions exist, you might want to look seriously at a third-party sale. Factors critical to a third-party sale include *determining the value of your business, knowing how to find a buyer,* and *structuring the sales transaction* from the seller's perspective.

Determining value and structure of the purchase are both critical elements of any transaction involving the transfer of stock, especially if you're planning on selling to co-owners or family members.

Determining a Value

Business owners often ask me and their accountants, "How much is my business worth?" I tell them the question is totally irrelevant and that a much better question would be "What is the most I can get for my business under the most favorable terms and conditions?"

Please realize that business valuation is a process that is absolutely nonabsolute. In fact, there are a number of different methods of valuing a closely held business, each involving a variety of factors with varying degrees of importance and each rendering a different value! I usually recommend an exercise that incorporates several techniques to arrive at a valuation *range*.

If an owner goes through this exercise well before the business is sold, he or she will be able to pinpoint the factors that are crucial to increasing the worth of the business. Your annual fiscal year-end meeting is a good time to revalue your business (see Chapter 2).

Surprisingly, one place to look for guidance is the IRS. In 1959 it issued Revenue Ruling 59-60. This ruling is still cited extensively today by the IRS when it places a value on your business. For our purposes it provides a useful starting point.

The major items listed by this revenue ruling are

- The nature of the business and its history from its inception.
- The general economic condition and outlook of the specific industry.
- The book value of the stock and the financial condition of the business.
- The earning capacity of the company.
- The dividend-paying capacity.
- Whether or not the enterprise has goodwill or other intangible value.
- Prior sales of the stock and size of the block of stock to be valued.
- The market price of stocks of corporations engaged in the same or similar line of business whose stocks are actively traded in a free and open market, either on an exchange or over-the-counter.

In addition to the IRS's valuation standards, the courts have over the years contributed their own ideas on how to determine a business's value. These include:

- Capitalization.
- Diversification of production.
- Labor policies.
- Quality of management.
- Importance of the selling owner to the success of the corporation.
- Net value of underlying assets.
- Prospects of creating a market for the stock.
- Restrictions on voting power or the transferability of the stock to be valued.

Other than simply *listing* these elements involved in arriving at a business value, neither the IRS nor the courts will tell you *which* of these factors carry more weight than the others in a particular business. That's as far as they go in providing guidance.

So far I think I've been a pretty good lawyer: I told you that your original question was irrelevant, but that it can be answered in an infinite variety of ways and there is no one correct answer. I've told you that both the IRS and the courts have come up with many ways to value your business. Now a good lawyer would say, "No more" and simply hand you the bill. However, unless you've borrowed this book from the library, you've already paid my bill. Therefore, let me try to give you some guidelines to wade through this morass and help you arrive at a reasonable valuation range for your own business. To do this, let's visit a junkyard in central Wyoming.

Marcus E. Hamilton Enterprises, Ltd., was so successful, it made me wonder why I didn't go into the junkyard business after high school rather than fritter away time in college and law school. Marcus, in his mid-fifties, had recently decided that southern Florida was more compatible with his winter lifestyle than central Wyoming. He also knew that there was no one in his junkyard business with either the savvy or finances to purchase his owner-ship interest. So when he met with us, he wanted some idea of what he might expect to receive upon the sale of his business to an outside third party.

First, we looked at the value of the assets within the business. This involved examining the book value of all assets, then adjusting those assets to fair market value. This is a necessary step if the cost of those assets, as reduced by accumulated depreciation, is not indicative of the true worth of the asset.

In the case of the junkyard business, this was particularly true. A wrecked pickup truck that might have been purchased for $50 could over time yield $1,000 worth of parts. Fortunately, Marcus kept good records (computerized, yet!) of the annual cost of purchased junks. Comparing that with the annual revenues, we were able to come up with a good adjusted fair market value of the original cost of the inventory.

The adjusted book value of his business looked like this:

Assets		*Liabilities*	
Real property	$ 118,479	Mortgages (real)	–0–
Equipment and fixtures	450,000	Mortgages (chattel)	–0–
		Loans (current)	$182,302
Inventory (adjusted for fair market value)	2,380,000	Accounts payable	138,954
		Notes payable	186,717
Accounts receivable	210,490	Deferred compensation	–0–
Notes receivable	750	Accrued taxes	6,252
Cash value life insurance	17,925	Other	3,973
Cash	–0–		
Prepaids and other	1,888		
Officer note	–0–		
Accrued interest	–0–		
Total assets	$3,179,532	Total liabilities	$518,198

Total assets:	$3,179,532
Less total liabilities:	518,198
Adjusted book value:	$2,661,334

The total fair market value of the assets (less liabilities) was $2,661,334. If Marcus did nothing but slowly liquidate his business, eventually he could expect to receive approximately that amount less the ongoing cost of operations. On the other hand, a quick liquidation would result in substantially less money than this because the cost of moving his inventory—hundreds of junked cars—would be too expensive and there was no immediate market for that many used cars in central Wyoming. Only by continuing the operation in place could Marcus realize maximum revenue.

After going through these calculations, we obtained one of the two numbers needed to come up with the full fair market value of the business—the net fair market value of the assets. Our evaluation work was, therefore, half completed. In addition to the net fair market value, we also needed to account for the *going concern value*.

Generally, the going concern value is also described as the "goodwill" or "blue sky" value of the business. It's a value beyond asset value. Reducing that value to a supportable number is more difficult and subjective than determining the fair market value of assets. The approach I like to take is the one most people would take when buying any income-producing asset. First I ask, What is the replacement value of the asset? Then I ask, What is the demonstrated earnings capacity of that asset?

If the earnings capacity is no greater than a reasonable yield or return on the fair market value of the assets, then there is no excess earnings capacity and no going concern value. On the other hand, if there are excess earnings, then there is a going concern value. To demonstrate this, study Exhibit 7-1. Try to work through it and then I'll explain it.

We arrived at a value of slightly more than $3 million as a sales price for this business. That amount is subject to several other considerations that we'll discuss below, but it is a supportable value. And it means more money in your pocket than if you were to sell on the basis of asset value or some unsupportable formula. To make it supportable, however, you

Exhibit 7-1. Going concern value.

---

(1) Average annual net earnings of the business: total compensation (including bonuses, personal use of corporate assets, and excess rents) paid to owners by the business plus the amount added to retained earnings or surplus of the business plus the amount of dividends paid to shareholders (the average annual net earnings of the previous three years is used with greater weight given to the most recent year and less to the initial year) ... $ 575,000

(2) Less estimated annual replacement salaries for all owners and their family members 65,000

(3) Less earnings on book value @ 17% annual return on $2,661,334 452,426

(4) Average net earnings due to "goodwill," past activity, and risk of capital [(1) above, minus (2) above, minus (3) above—$575,000 − $65,000 − $452,426] 57,574

(5) Multiply (4) above × 6 years 345,444

(6) Add the adjusted book value 2,661,334

(7) Total value [(5) + (6)] $3,006,778

---

need to understand how we arrived at each of the line item totals.

First, the *average annual net earnings* of the business is computed. You have considerable flexibility in determining "average." You can decide to go back one year or five years. You can give greater weight to the more recent years or simply have a true average of all years under consideration. This becomes part of your bargaining or negotiation when you begin discussions with a potential buyer.

Purchasers are interested in the *trend* of earnings history, and they will invariably give greater consideration to more current earnings of the business. For this reason greater weight must be given to more recent earnings history to obtain a realistic earning "average." If your earnings history has been stable for many years, it will reflect that increased value under line item (5) by increasing the number of years—the capitalization rate in effect—of the annual net earnings.

Purchasers also want to know how much money the owner has really been taking out of the business. That's why it's critical to *recast* the financial information of the company to give the buyer that understanding.

Prudent tax planning for the business owner means that his use of the company's income stream has involved more than simply drawing a salary and, perhaps, a bonus. The planning can involve a variety of other factors, such as leasing personally owned assets to the company in return for high rent, the use of medical expense reimbursement plans, making highly favorable retirement plan contributions, using company assets such as cars and airplanes, and employing a spouse and children at higher-than-expected salaries or wages.

All these amounts must be recast as earnings available to the business owner. It behooves you, then, to start now with your accountant to keep track of these excess earnings.

In line item (2) of the chart, the net earnings are reduced by the *estimated replacement salaries* after your departure. What will it cost to replace you? The answer will be found by looking to industry standards, the salaries paid to key members of your management team now in place, and to what you think is sensible. With the exception of professional service businesses, replacement salaries are usually not a significant factor in arriving at the total value of the business.

In item (3), earnings on book value are multiplied by a percentage amount. Theoretically, this amount can be anything you want it to be. Realistically, it's the rate of return a reasonable person would want on his capital, subject to the risk factors of that capital. In other words, if I were to loan your business $100,000 to buy inventory, what rate of return would I insist upon having to cover the possibility that you might default on that loan?

Keep in mind also that my loan would be subordinated to any type of bank financing available. Consequently, this rate of return must be higher than any outstanding indebtedness the business has with any financial institution. Typically, a reasonable person (especially the potential buyer of your business) would want a rate of return between 15 percent and 20 percent.

The greater the return expected on the assets, the lower the going concern value of the business. The percentage in this line item will decrease if there is a stable earnings history, if the company has been in business for many years, and if the assets are readily salable.

Other factors unique to your business may affect the upward or downward movement of that percentage rate. Again, it's in your best interest to begin a list of those reasons supporting a lower percentage rate. The list would indicate the amount of risk an investor would have if he put money into your business. Obviously, this rate would never go below the rate on long-term treasury bonds. A rate much higher than 25 percent normally results in the business having no going concern value.

Line item (4), earnings on goodwill, computes the effect of goodwill. It's what is left over after everything else has been taken from the earnings.

Line (5) multiplies the net annual earnings on goodwill by an amount of years. For Marcus E. Hamilton Enterprises, Ltd., that number of years was six. How did we arrive at that number? Much of our analysis was similar in nature to looking at what rate of return an investor would want if he invested in the assets of the company. In closely held businesses the multiple can range from zero to ten. A typical range is two to five times the annual excess earnings capacity or going concern value.

One way of looking at this is to ask, For how many years would a new owner be willing to give you the excess earnings capacity of the business in order to purchase that earnings capacity from you? As in the analysis to determine the required earnings on book value (line item (3) above), the first factor is risk. Here the risk is the ability of the business to continue to earn excess amounts above the expected rate of return on the book value. In most businesses that risk is greater than the book value. For Marcus's firm, the book value rate of

17 percent translates to a capitalization rate of about 6 (6 times earnings of $452,426 equals $2,714,556).

In computing the risk multiple with respect to the excess earnings capacity, the analysis must include five factors. We'll discuss each in turn.

1. *The degree to which the excess earnings are transferable to the buyer.* In other words, what do you take with you when you leave the business?

In the case of Marcus's company, the answer was very little. The earnings of the company were based on the inventory—the junked cars—not Marcus's unique abilities. On the other hand, the ability to transfer earnings capacity to a new owner would be much more difficult for a small manufacturing representative's business with one or two employees, little or no inventory, and where all relationships with both customers and the manufacturer's lines were maintained by the owner. That's why you can often get more money by finding a co-owner or employee who has the ability to continue the relationships while buying you out.

In earlier chapters we discussed creating business value. If you are unable to have in place a strong organization structure that can exist and thrive independently of you, you may be able to look only to the adjusted book value of the business for valuation purposes. Sometimes this can be enough (see the construction company example in Chapter 1). But for businesses that are not capital intensive, excess earnings capacity is the primary component of value. If that's your situation now, you must do everything possible while you are still active in the business to ensure the permanency of that earnings capacity.

2. *History of profitability.* This is self-evident. I would only add that a stable earnings history, as opposed to a "peaky" earnings history, is more reassuring to the prospective buyer and his advisors.

3. *Market share.* Most closely held businesses will not dominate their market. However, with Marcus E. Hamilton

Enterprises, Ltd., that was not the case. Marcus had a lock on the junkyard business for an area of several hundred square miles. He was not only an important source of junk parts, but his business was the first one thought of when it came to disposing of unwanted vehicles.

How dominant in your market is your business? In answering this question, it helps to determine first just what is your market. For example, I have a friend who owns a much smaller junkyard in a major metropolitan area. Yet he too is a dominant player in the market. In his case the market is Mustang and Camaro used parts. The total number of his junk cars is perhaps 5 percent of Marcus's. But in the Mustang and Camaro used parts market, my friend has a much higher percentage, even in the more populous metro area. And this places a premium on the value of this business.

4. *Industry trends.* These can be important if your business is in an industry clearly in decline or is a front-runner in the current hot technology. Otherwise, trends are not terribly relevant.

However, the location of your business could be a factor. For example, while Marcus's original business location was far away from civilization (even as that term is loosely defined in Wyoming), over the last twenty years a town grew up within sight of his junkyard. This has served to increase the value of his business for two reasons: He's closer to his customers, and any would-be competitors would have a hard time getting zoning approval for another junkyard so close to town.

5. *Items unique to the business.* For example, another client has been the printer for a weekly newspaper for more than fifteen years. While there is no written contract, the newspaper has become very reliant on my client. A change to another printer would be costly and time-consuming. Thus, a new owner would be assured of a continuing, profitable revenue stream—unless he totally mucked it up. Most businesses, however, do not benefit from long-term contracts. Our economy and business practices have become more competitive and fluid in recent years, and in a fast-paced, fast-changing

business world, long-term contracts and relationships have a lesser role to play.

There may be similar factors in your own business, which should go into this formula determination. I hope the above discussion persuades you to avoid blindly using any "industry standards" in valuing your business. Often we have clients tell us, "Well, my business is worth the gross annual revenues," because that is what they have read or heard from friends in their industry. At best, those "industry standards" provide only useful comparisons to a more proper valuation. At worst, they are misleading and an obstacle that must be overcome in presenting your value to a prospective purchaser. There is a real value difference between a company grossing $1 million and earning $50,000, and a company in the same industry earning $150,000 in profit on the same revenues.

A final note on Marcus E. Hamilton Enterprises, Ltd. In arriving at the value for his business, we wanted to be reasonable, yet optimistic. We did not ignore negative factors, which would exert downward pressure on the value. Going through the valuation formula well before selling the business enabled us to highlight the important areas and concentrate Marcus's business efforts on areas that would enhance his valuation.

The above example, though lengthy, is elementary. In my experience, it does account for the two primary components of business valuation—the true value of the underlying assets and the excess earnings capacity (going concern value) of the business.

By going through the exercise at the end of this chapter, you will discover the areas of your business that need additional attention in order to maximize value under this formula. I think you will find the exercise worthwhile, even if you have no immediate plans to sell.

Using Other Advisors to Value Your Business

When the decision is actually made to sell your business, it's critical that you consult with your accountant, your attorney, and perhaps your financial planner. Undoubtedly, you will get suggestions regarding valuation techniques to be used for your business. In addition, you and your advisors should determine if it is necessary to hire a business appraiser to formally value your company. Involving a good independent business appraiser early in the process can help to maximize the value of your company. He can help not only on the current value, but also on ways to enhance it under specific formulas and valuation techniques.

Finding the Buyer

While finding a buyer can often be as difficult as finding a snip of hay in a mound of needles, some businesses are continually approached by potential purchasers. Your business will fall in the latter category if you follow the essential guidelines below.

Selling Your Business to Someone Familiar With It

Criminologists say that most murderers know their victims. That's good news for people who have few enemies or travel in friendly circles. Similarly, you probably already know who will purchase your business. The buyer is likely to be your fellow competitor, one of your suppliers, a major customer, or someone who has heard of your business through those sources.

Sometimes you will know these people well enough to tell them you are interested in selling. Often they will sense you are ready to leave business by watching your level of interest in the day-to-day operations of the business. That's why it's critical that you always present your business operation in the best possible light to those competitors, suppliers, and customers.

When I speak of competitors, I don't necessarily mean those in your immediate trade area. Instead, a potential purchaser is often a fellow competitor who is active in your national trade or industry organization. It's much easier to be open with someone in a similar line of business in a different locality. They, or people they know, may be interested in expanding to your area. They will be familiar with your type of business. They may well have known you, or least heard of you, for years before any sale takes place.

Again, if you're interested in selling at a future date, but are not active in your national industry organization, I suggest you think about joining. You may find the buyer of your business at that organization's next function.

In a similar vein, national suppliers are often interested in acquiring company-owned stores. Although their marketing plans seem to change direction with each management change, large companies that franchise their retail operations or give territorial rights for the sale of their products are often interested in acquiring a sound local operation. Whether it's a restaurant franchise or a tire distributorship, large companies are especially interested in those operations whose loss or defection to a different supplier or manufacturer would adversely affect the national company's revenues from your area.

Finally, large users of your services or products may decide that acquiring your business would be less expensive than either continuing to use your business on a contract basis or starting a similar subsidiary of their own. Obviously this carries with it both a risk and a reward. You could lose all of your business if they started their own subsidiary based on confidential information they obtained while considering the purchase of your business. An alternative would be to sell your business to another financially strong company.

Using Your Advisors

Our clients frequently ask us if we know of anyone who would be interested in buying their businesses. Conversely, we have clients who ask if we know of any businesses for sale. Normally we are of little use in the context of a "business broker." On the other hand, several national accounting firms are offering, on a seemingly informal basis, to market your business through their offices throughout the country.

The effectiveness of this form of business marketing has yet to be demonstrated to my satisfaction. If you're considering using outside individuals to help sell your business, I suggest a business broker.

I view business brokers as most people view lawyers: a necessary evil. No one likes to use a business broker. They charge a fee and therefore usually become involved only after your own less formal efforts to locate a buyer have proved unsuccessful. Typically, brokers charge 10 percent to 12 percent to sell a business worth less than $500,000, and about 10 percent for a business sold for less than $1 million. For large deals a sliding scale is used. Often that scale is 8 percent for the first million, 6 percent for the second million, 4 percent for the third million, and 2 percent thereafter. On sales of businesses worth over $10 million, the fee is negotiated.

As in every profession or trade, there are good business brokers—and all others. To find a good one, you should again look to your trade or business organization to see if there are brokers who specialize and are known in your industry. Once you find one, demand references. Have your CPA interview the broker. In the end it will be to your advantage to go through this process and choose a national business brokerage if your business cannot easily be sold to local concerns because of uniqueness, value, or you desire to ensure privacy.

It's also possible to sell your business by advertising it in trade publications, national business newspapers and magazines, or local newspapers. However, this technique has not been successful with any of my clients.

A word about *secrecy*. Any serious potential purchaser will insist on seeing all of your recent financial records as a first step. Thereafter, if still interested, he will want to see *all of your other operating files*—contracts, employee manuals and procedures, customer lists, and more. In short, the potential purchaser will want to know as much about your business as you do.

With that knowledge goes the very real risk that it can be

used against you should the deal fall through, especially if the potential buyer is a competitor or would-be competitor. The knowledge he gains about your company could enable him to approach a similar business and make a precise, lower offer.

So how do you protect yourself? You use methods to reduce your exposure—confidentiality agreements, letters of intent, and option contracts.

Confidentiality agreements prevent use of the information from being used in any way other than to determine whether or not to purchase your business. Letters of intent define the basis for agreement, without intending to be a legal commitment to follow through with an agreement. They can often be more of a problem than a solution; if the negotiations break down, one party may try to enforce the letter against the other.

If a legally binding agreement is called for, a written purchase agreement subject to certain contingencies may be drawn up. An option contract is binding if certain contingencies are met, such as the ability of the buyer to obtain financing, the gaining of your bank or franchisor's consent to the sale, and the confirmation of the accuracy of representations you've made.

Because protection of your business secrets should not be underestimated, it's equally important that you exercise your own "due diligence" with respect to the potential buyer. Before releasing financial and other information, you have the right to determine the buyer's ability to purchase by requiring financial assurances from him.

You should make every reasonable effort to check out the references of the prospective purchaser for honesty as well as from a financial standpoint. Often it's easier for your advisors to conduct this investigation than it is for you. It is always more comfortable to blame your lawyer for overzealousness than it is to accept the responsibility yourself. And we lawyers are accustomed to being cast as the "bad guys." Some of us rather enjoy it.

With the help of your advisors, you should prepare a proposal letter setting forth the basic terms of the deal. These terms would include the purchase price, the amount you are willing to carry, your willingness to remain with the business for a period of time during the transition of the ownership, and other pertinent details.

In that letter basic financial information can probably be disclosed without undue harm to you, although it's always a good idea to get a confidentiality agreement. The information would include annual revenues, profitability, ownership structure, and fair market value of the assets. Based on that proposal letter—if interest exists and the ability to purchase is present—then a confidentality agreement should be signed by the prospective buyer before he receives detailed financial and other information.

The use of a business broker can also help maintain confidentiality. Through him, you may divulge full financial and other details while withholding the name and precise location of your business. This allows the brokerage company to disseminate information to a broad range of potential purchasers (who have been prescreened as to financial capability) without jeopardizing the confidentiality of your business.

Structuring the Sale

You can help ensure a successful sale by answering the following four questions: (1) What is it that I'm selling? (2) How am I going to be paid? (3) How can I minimize my income tax consequences, and (4) How will the actual selling process be conducted?

Let's examine each.

What Are You Selling?

An early determination of exactly what it is you're selling is critical in determining the ultimate sale price, the tax consequences of the sale, and your involvement with the business once the sale has closed.

A third-party buyer will generally prefer to buy assets rather than stock not only for tax reasons, but also to protect himself from the contingent or unknown liabilities of your business. When the business interest is sold as a whole in the form of a stock sale, the purchaser acquires all the assets *and* liabilities. Unlike the key employee or co-owner, the third-party purchaser will not be as familiar with the business history and consequently will be more reluctant to buy stock. But the tax cost of selling assets may be high, in effect a double tax, as mentioned below.

This issue—the sale of assets vs. stock—may be subject to extensive negotiations. The following categories of assets are normally sold:

- The furniture, fixtures, equipment, and supplies used in the ongoing business.
- The inventory, if any.
- The current telephone number of your business (particularly important if you are a personal service business, or a retail business that advertises heavily).
- Customer lists and records (especially important where a large part of the value attributable to the business lies in these records—a general medical or dental practice, for example).
- The covenant not to compete limited by time, scope, and perhaps geographical boundary (see Chapter 2).
- Leasehold improvements.
- Accounts receivable.
- Real estate, if applicable.

You also sell the going concern value, or goodwill. This is often represented in the form of a consulting agreement, or deferred compensation agreement, as well as a covenant not to compete. Nevertheless, the amount paid for goodwill should be separately determined and only then allocated to specific assets or contracts. This is important in order not to diminish the value you would otherwise receive for those assets or for service performed under these contracts.

Often a prudent purchaser will insist that you remain active in the business for a period of time after the closing.

This can be important to the buyer in order to maintain relationships with customers, suppliers, and employees, as well as to help train and educate the new owners in the details of the business.

If you're going to spend time in the business after selling it, make certain your responsibilities are precisely defined—the number of hours you'll work each week, and for how many weeks, and the amount of compensation you'll receive for your services.

It's also nice to have your employment agreement contain a severance clause that allows you to end the relationship at any time in return for a "declining penalty" payment by you. In other words, if you find the ownership to be impossible to work with—as many entrepreneurs do no matter how good the new ownership is—make sure you have a provision that permits you to terminate your employment without causing a default of the overall purchase agreement.

Frequently the new owners, if they feel a need to retain your services, will insist on structuring your employment agreement in such a way that a major portion of your proceeds from the sale of your business will be paid only if you remain with the company and *if* the company continues to perform to expectations.

When I represent a purchaser, I usually attempt to retain the services of any key personnel/owners and, at the same time, make them toe the line on the performance projections they gave our purchaser when the sale was negotiated. If performance declines, so does the purchase price.

Retaining the former owner as an employee becomes less important if the business to be sold already has a strong management team and organization structure in place with a proven track record. These considerations involving your services are also less important if the major portion of the sales price is represented by an asset liquidation sale as opposed to a sale based on the going concern value.

A few words about the sale of real estate are appropriate here. Business owners frequently own the real estate on which the business is conducted. Usually they want to sell the

property along with the business. However, the typical purchaser doesn't have enough cash to buy both the business and
the real estate. When that happens, the seller might consider
a long-term lease—perhaps with an option to purchase down
the road—between the seller and the business, personally
guaranteed by the buyer.

This makes the purchase more affordable to the buyer
and, if something goes wrong during the buyout period, the
real property can remain separate from any difficulties that
may otherwise be encountered.

How Am I Going to Be Paid?

One way of getting paid is to be cashed out in full. If that
happens, you have located not a snip of hay but a bouquet of
roses in a mountain of needles. If you are not so fortunate—
sellers of closely held businesses seldom are—you will be
required to carry back some of the purchase price, probably
subordinated to bank financing.

At this point the "deals" begin to vary considerably. As a
general rule, some type of carryback is necessary in almost all
circumstances. Even when a bank would be willing to finance
the entire purchase price, it will often require you to carry
back 15 percent to 30 percent, or more, subordinated to the
bank.

This provides the bank with the same amount of security
as a lower loan amount. At the same time, it ensures your
continuing interest in the affairs of the business. This attitude
of the bank is more prevalent where part of the purchase price
is represented by the going concern value. In short, to the
extent the bank's loan is not covered by the hard assets of the
business, you can expect to carry the balance.

Typically, the amount of your carry will be from 20
percent to 50 percent of the total price. If you recall, where
employees, co-owners, or family members are involved in the
purchase, the amount of your carry is often more significant.

In a third-party sale, however, your control will not be as
great, and your knowledge of the ability and attitude of the

purchaser probably will be limited. Consequently, you must minimize your risk by getting as much of the purchase price up front as possible.

In receiving payment of the sales price, consider the following:

- *The amount of the earnest money deposit, if any, you should receive at the time the contract is signed.* This amount is normally refundable if the deal does not close for reasons beyond the control of the purchaser. Those terms are spelled out in the purchase contract.

- *The amount to be paid in cash at closing.*

- *The amount of the promissory note, the interest rate, and the payback period.* Consider a floating interest rate, one or two points over prime. That rate is usually at least as good as any rate the purchaser will likely find. The payback period should be kept as short as possible—determined by the purchaser's ability to afford the payments.

- *The amount and type of collateral that will be satisfactory to you.* A deed of trust or mortgage should be used to secure any real estate. A uniform commercial code security agreement and financing statement should be used to secure the furniture, fixtures, equipment, and accounts receivable.

- *Outside collateral.* Real estate or other assets owned by the purchaser can be encumbered. Although the personal guarantee of the purchaser and his spouse is mandated in all but the rarest of situations, an outside guarantor should also be considered—a form of "F&F financing." ("F&F" stands for friends and family.) A personal guarantee is not worth a lot if the personal assets of the guarantor are nonexistent. I often recommend to clients who are selling their professional practices—medical or dental—to a young doctor or dentist that they secure the personal guarantee not only of the professional, but also of his parent.

- *The inclusion of a prepayment penalty.* This is especially important when part of your payment is deferred compensation. With the constant tinkering of the tax code by

Congress, no one can ever tell whether tax rates will increase or decrease markedly from one year to the next. The inclusion of a prepayment penalty prevents the seller from paying large amounts of deferred compensation to you in a particular year in order to take advantage of high income tax brackets—a deduction for the company, but taxable income for you.

    • *Tax consequences.* These are generally no different than if you sell your business to your employees or co-owners. (Chapter 6 discusses the differences between a sale of stock only, or the sale of stock combined with deferred compensation, consulting agreement, use of accelerated retirement plan contributions, and use of an ESOP to help pay for your business interest.)

How Can I Minimize My Income Tax Consequences?

Generally, a sale of corporate assets (other than from an S Corporation) will involve a double tax consequence to the seller. First, the corporation will recognize gain on the sale of the assets and then the owner will also recognize gain when he receives money from the corporation as a result of that sale.

    Use of compensation arrangements, deferred compensation, or consulting or noncompete agreements can remove some of the sting from the double tax bite. Nevertheless, a double tax on any amount of gain is a painful experience. Have your CPA calculate the tax consequences both ways: the consequences of a straight stock sale and those of a sale of assets and liquidation of the company. Occasionally a sale of assets is not painful. This is true when the basis of the assets within the company is high or when the basis of your ownership interest in the company approaches the total purchase price of the asset sale.

How Will the Actual Selling Process Be Conducted?

In most cases, the sales process generally follows this course of action:

1. Prenegotiations.
2. Negotiations with the buyer.
3. Legal considerations.
4. Determination of last-minute contingencies.
5. Determination of your duties during transition of ownership.
6. Determination of the warranties and representations you will provide.
7. Closing of the deal.

Let's look at each.

• *The pre-negotiation phase* occurs before a firm offer has been made for your company. Before you enter this phase, you should know your objectives—both financial and "human." Ask yourself, How much money do I want or need? How much am I willing to carry? Do I want to continue to be active in the business? Do I want to be able to start a new, competing business? Am I willing to relinquish all management control when I sell this business?

Your answers to these questions will dictate the terms you require to close the deal.

You must also determine the strategy you'll employ with a potential purchaser. The strategy may vary from buyer to buyer. For example, what aspects of the valuation formula do you wish to emphasize? This part of the strategy is usually designed by your advisors.

In addition to performing the functions described earlier in this chapter, your advisors will also help you determine the asking price of your business. Using your advisors at this point tends to minimize the cost to you of selling. If you wait until you've struck a deal before calling on your advisors, it may be more expensive, especially if your earlier decisions are irrevocable and wrong.

• *Negotiating with the buyer* requires basic negotiating techniques. I like to negotiate face-to-face with potential purchasers if my client is a solid and successful owner. As a successful businessperson, you've probably already acquired good negotiating skills. You know more about your business than your buyer does. If you use good advisors, you've assembled a formidable team and you'll be better prepared to deal than the purchaser. In face-to-face negotiations your team will be able to gauge and respond to the true concerns of the buyer and answer his questions immediately.

In this phase it's important to establish and maintain your credibility. Don't peg your asking price unreasonably high or make representations of future performance that cannot possibly be supported by your company's earnings and revenue history.

Perhaps most important of all, *know your bottom line.* These are the minimum terms you require to make the deal. The terms should have been determined in the prenegotiation phase—before you ever met the potential buyer. In addition to the purchase price, your bottom line must include the terms of your carryback and the maximum extent of your continued involvement in the company after closing.

Finally, *control your personality.* Don't try to drive too hard a bargain. Be cordial and businesslike and, above all, be patient. *Several rounds of negotiations are normal;* you should not expect to sit down at the negotiating table and hammer out all the details of the sale in a few hours.

• *The legal considerations* we discussed earlier in this chapter under "Structuring the Sale" are usually predominant after the initial negotiating sessions. At this time your attorney should draft the purchase contract, taking into account all the elements described earlier as well as the determination of how the sales price is going to be paid.

Notice that I said *your* attorney should prepare this contract, *not the buyer's lawyer.* Don't think that you'll save legal fees by allowing the other side to prepare the contract. What invariably comes back if the buyer's lawyer draws up the agreement is one tailored to the wishes of the purchaser and his attorney. You're better off putting all your requests in the initial document and then allowing the buyer to whittle away at them or try to add specific provisions.

• *Contingencies will come up prior to or at the closing.* Your advisors will want to keep these at a minimum. Normally, they would include only the securing of financing by the purchaser. An evaluation by your banker or CPA of the purchaser's financial statement—and your business's financial statement—will allow you to evaluate the financing ability of the prospective buyer.

You must also obtain your landlord's consent to the assignment of your office or business lease to the buyer. Ask the landlord to release you totally from any contingent liability under the lease. He'll probably refuse. Ordinarily there's nothing you can do about that except seek indemnification from the purchaser. At least you can try. Similarly, you need to assign any equipment leases to the buyer. Again, this is ordinarily not a problem.

Finally, the buyer must acquire any necessary licenses and permits to conduct your business.

• *Your duties during the transition period* must be determined. After the closing has occurred, you may or may not continue as an employee or consultant of the new ownership. However, it's common to expect some continued involvement in the business even in situations in which you are cashed out. This means introducing the new owner to all key players: suppliers, customers, employees, bankers, and others.

• *Warranties and representations* are other items that always survive the closing of the sale. Usually you'll be required to give these when the purchase agreement is first signed. Naturally you and your advisors will seek to limit the warranties you give. Common warranties the buyer asks for are listed in the seller's Warranties and Representations Exhibit at the end of this chapter. Review them well before any purchase occurs. By knowing what to expect, you'll be better prepared to respond.

It's likely there will be additional warranties and representations required of you that are unique to your business. For example, if you are a medical doctor, you may be asked to guarantee the number of your active patient files.

• *Closing the deal* will require adjustments to the purchase price. Count on it. These are typically standard changes
of little consequence to either you or the buyer. They involve
things like insurance premiums, rent and security deposits,
utility company deposits, employee benefits, payroll and payroll taxes, and personal property taxes due for the year of
closing.

Summary

There are many elements involved in the successful sale of
your company to a third party. The seeds of that sale are
almost always sown long before the sale occurs. Creating value
for your ownership interest is the first step. The second is
determining that value in accordance with the process described in this chapter. The sales process for your business
begins the day you acquire it and does not end until the day
you receive final payment. The sales process is completed
when you find a buyer and structure a deal under satisfactory
terms and conditions.

The warranties and representations listed next are typical
of most business sales. You can expect additional warranties
and representations based upon the particular circumstances
of your sales transaction. As the seller you will want to limit
their extent and number. However, be prepared to accurately
respond to the following.

SELLER'S WARRANTIES AND REPRESENTATIONS

☐ That the financial information previously supplied by seller to
buyer is true and accurate and was prepared in accordance with
"generally accepted standard accounting principles consistently
applied."

☐ Nothing has come to the attention of seller that can reasonably be
interpreted to result in any material adverse change in the seller's
financial condition.

☐ There is no reason not to believe that the majority of seller's patients/clients/customers/vendors and referral sources will continue to do business with the buyer following the closing, and there has been no loss or threatened loss of seller's patients/clients/customers/vendors.

☐ The execution of the agreement does not violate any provision of any agreement to which seller is a party.

☐ Seller has valid title to all of the assets to be sold to buyer.

☐ All taxes that seller is required to pay have been paid, and seller does not have any tax deficiencies proposed or assessed against seller.

☐ To the best of seller's knowledge, there are no suits or proceedings pending or threatened against seller or any of the properties or assets used by seller.

☐ Between signing the contract and closing, seller will not make any material changes in the business outside the ordinary course of business and will exert his best efforts to keep and make available the services of the present employees and preserve the goodwill of patients/clients/customers.

☐ Seller is not a party to any contract for the purchase of materials, supplies, equipment, or fixtures that will survive the date of closing.

☐ Seller will comply with the "Bulk Sales Act."

☐ There is no material error, misstatement, or omission in the representations and warranties of seller or in any certificate or document given by seller.

☐ All representations and warranties made by the seller shall be true and accurate as of the closing and shall survive the closing.

☐ There are no liabilities against seller of any nature that would affect seller's right to sell assets to buyer.

☐ The assets being sold shall be in good working condition at closing.

8

"Dad Always Liked You Best!"—Part I

Transferring ownership to your children

The most popular television soap operas of the 1980s—"Dallas," "Falcon Crest," "Dynasty," "Knots Landing"—all were big, brawling stories set in the context of a family-run business enterprise. Why? Because conflict among family members provides an endless variety of dramatic material for the scriptwriter. Sadly, in my practice I've seen what conflict can do to real family-owned businesses.

Instead of being brought together by working side-by-side in a family-operated business, too many families wind up being torn apart, sometimes irreversibly.

There are countless situations that produce this conflict, but most problems begin when children are brought into the business with the expectation they will take it over one day. While there are many reasons why ownership transfer to another party can be unsuccessful, transfer to a younger generation contains not only all of the same risks and dangers, but additional ones as well. In fact, the risk is infinitely greater.

Subjective Elements in the Family-Run Business

In a family situation more is involved than mere economic loss. In extreme cases the risk could mean the severing of family ties and relationships forever. And the possibility of such a devastating result is greater because of the subjective elements that exist in the family-run business.

Here are some common scenarios:

1. The business owner feels a need to transfer his interest to one or more of his children for less than fair market value. This then leads to the owner's desire to be "fair and equal" to other sons or daughters who are not active in the business and therefore do not receive any gifts of stock in that business.

2. The owner allows children to become owners when they first enter the business even though they may lack the experience, intelligence, ambition, or motivation to warrant such responsibility. Later they become the controlling owners. I've frequently observed that the less able the child, the more blind the otherwise capable business owner is to his child's weaknesses. In fact, there is an inverse relationship—the greater the child's inability to manage and run the business, the more likely he is to be placed in management. This occurs most often when the business owner has achieved unusual success due to the force of his own personality.

3. The owner gives operating control or transfers ownership to offspring at the expense of more experienced, more capable, more worthy employees, who had the misfortune of not being the owner's son or daughter.

4. The owner hires his children, who have been engaged in ongoing sibling rivalry. They continue that rivalry; only now the war is taking place not only at home, but inside the business.

5. The owner permits family members who are not active in the business to decide such things as when, to whom, and how much should be transferred to the family members. Ordinarily this is the business owner's spouse, who is deter-

mined to make sure all of his or her children are treated absolutely equally, regardless of their contribution to the business.

6. The owner transfers control to a son or daughter before his own retirement objectives are met; or conversely, he waits too long to begin the transfer process, thereby making it impossible to avoid substantial estate taxes on the value of his stock at his death.

As you can see, disaster awaits the owners who fail to take certain required steps: to set their objectives and a firm timetable, to make and implement needed decisions, and to obtain the consent of all affected family members.

Incredibly, sometimes an owner manages to neglect every step. This reminds me of the Rumler family.

How Not *to Do It!*

George Rumler's accountant arranged for me to meet George to discuss the future of his company, Rumler & Sons Mould and Die Company, a plastic injection molding company. George started the company in the early 1950s, and it had grown steadily, ultimately employing twenty-five people, including his four sons. Two other children were not active in the business.

The four sons, in their late twenties or thirties, had joined the business either out of high school or college. One or two had quit the company, only to return later. While Dad owned a majority of the stock of the company and was its president, he had turned daily operating control over to Ned, his second oldest son. Ned was the most capable of the children—and the least liked.

Dale was the oldest son. As such, he felt he should be running the business. Instead, he was working as an outside salesman, and his performance lagged behind that of even the newest sales personnel.

John, the youngest son, was in charge of production. He was capable and a hard worker, but immature and temperamental. He was also his mother's favorite.

Then there was Paul, also a salesman. He had a drug problem, and often failed to show up for work for days on end.

All four sons received a salary based on their living needs, rather than on their positions of responsibility and their value to the company, and each sought the favor of their father in an attempt to gain ultimate control of the business at his retirement or death.

To make matters worse, each owned a different amount of stock, given to the sons when they entered the business. And there was no written buy-and-sell agreement among them to govern or restrict the transferability of stock.

The elder Rumler, the founder and owner, looked around one day and realized he had a lot of problems. He was tired of work and of putting up with the constant bickering and complaints of his sons which, in turn, were leading the business in a downward spiral as the sons expended more time maneuvering for power bases than performing work.

George wanted to retire, but the only way he could get enough money to do so was to sell his stock to his children. However, none of them wanted to buy his stock without being able to control the business. Moreover, they would need to look to the revenues of the business to provide for the purchase price, and because of the downward trend of the business, adequate revenues could not be forecast to provide funds for the buyout.

Adding to the problem was the attitude of George's wife. She was determined that two other children—not involved in the business—should receive equal treatment.

Could a scenario like this actually exist? In fact, it did, and it eventually led to the end of the business. Ned, the most capable son, left the company after suing his father and three brothers. The elder Rumler was never able to retire—even though he'd reached retirement age—because of the inability of his other sons to run the business. Other lawsuits were filed, either by the company or the sons, charging each other with theft, breach of fiduciary duty, and similar allegations. Meanwhile, the best and most experienced employees left as soon as they could find other jobs, the quality of the company's products suffered, and customers began leaving.

The business was permanently ruined. Eventually, George just shut the doors.

It is easy to look back and see why things went haywire. George had failed to *set objectives*, to establish a *timetable* for transition and control from him to his sons, to *make decisions*, *obtain consensus* and agreement, *communicate* effectively to all family members to achieve understanding of his objectives and, finally, to *implement* his decisions.

Without all this, the ultimate results were inevitable. It was a textbook example of how lack of ownership planning could shut down a successful company.

The Decision-Making Process

Before we go on to discuss the specific techniques to use in transferring ownership to your children, let's first examine the decision-making process leading up to such a transfer. As we've seen, George Rumler failed miserably at each step in that process.

To arrive at your destination, it helps to know where you are going. To achieve your objectives, you have to know *exactly* what they are. It's not enough to say—in a general way—that you want to retire comfortably someday while giving your business to your children. That's too vague; specific objectives must be established. This dictates the decision-making process that includes the following five areas.

1. Determining How Much Money You Want From the Business

The amount of money you want from the business may be a combination of current salary, deferred salary or compensation to be paid out in your retirement years, money for your stock, increased rents for business property you may continue to own after the transfer, increased retirement plan contributing during your remaining working years, or any number of other sources.

At this point, it's not important to determine the method of getting the money out. Your advisors will do that for you. What *is* important is to determine how *much money* you want or need—in total—from your business.

Once you have determined how much money you will need, other questions should be addressed. These might include, Which of your children will become active in the business? Which key employees might become co-owners with your children? What new direction would you like your business to take as you ease away from managing the company yourself? How much continued involvement will be required of you? For how long? And in what areas of the business?

2. What Is Your Timetable?

Now that you've determined *where* you are headed, you must establish *when* you want to arrive there. Establishing a timetable is indispensable to a successful transfer of ownership to your children. Here's why:

A well thought out timetable forces you to determine not only when critical events must occur, but what those events are. These would include attaining certain financial objectives such as having enough money in a retirement plan, savings account, or investments outside the business. It might also include attaining certain business objectives relating to profitability, revenue or sales, or other standards indicating a stable and growing company—such as hiring your first sales manager or controller. These are especially important if much of your funds will come from business revenue after you become inactive in the business.

3. What Is Your Ownership Structure?

Normally, while the owner is actively involved with the company, its ownership structure is simple: He owns it all. Frankly, that is the ideal ownership arrangement—one owner, in absolute control, bearing all of the risk and all the reward of the business. For a variety of reasons, that simplest of structures must change as the business owner begins to transfer ownership to his child or children. The reasons for this can be many.

First, the very act of transferring stock to a child means

there will be at least one more shareholder. Often, two or more offspring become co-owners. Second, it's often appropriate to include key employees in the new stock ownership arrangement, especially if they are deserving and the children are incapable of running the business without the help of the key employees.

Third, different parts of the business may be transferred to different children. For example, one of my clients owned a manufacturing company with two locations, each making a different product line. As part of his planning, we decided to transfer one operation to his son and the other, smaller, operation to a valuable, long-term employee. Our client kept the original corporation and, in effect, turned it into a leasing company. He leased the real property and equipment to his son and the key employee, creating important advantages.

The most common situation, outside of transferring the entire business interest to one child, is to transfer it to two or more children. Does this have the potential for family discord?

The jealousy between siblings dates from Cain and Abel. It's a theme that fascinates us today. Perhaps that's why we watch television's "Dallas" and similar programs. Because the rivalry between brothers and sisters is often so intense, it may be prudent to consider splitting business divisions into distinctly separate companies and giving each child sole ownership of a division. If that is unworkable, then it's imperative to establish a solid organizational structure, giving each child definitive, written job descriptions and responsibilities. In addition, a thorough business continuity agreement must be provided—one that contains provisions to independently resolve business disputes and irreconcilable conflicts among the children. The purpose of this agreement is fully discussed in Chapter 9.

4. Obtaining Consensus for the Plan

You have determined your objectives, set your timetable, and structured the new ownership arrangements. Now comes the most difficult task: You must obtain a consensus from all the affected parties. These people include—first and foremost—your spouse, the children who will be active in the business, the children who will *not* be active, and, finally, your key employees.

Often I find owners attempting to obtain a consensus before they have worked through the earlier steps. They do this for a personal, subjective reason. They don't want to hurt the feelings of other family members or key employees by excluding them from the decision-making process. As an expression of familial love, this motive is laudable. As a process to effectively transfer control to a younger generation, it is wrong, wrong, wrong!

If you attempt to formulate a plan with your family members participating in the decision making, you may not be able to please all the members. In fact, it's most unlikely.

For example, a child who is not actively participating in the business may object to the lifetime transfer of stock to his siblings who are in the business while he receives nothing until your death. If the siblings participate on an equal basis in the forming of the business continuity plan they may, in effect, have a veto power over that plan because of their relationship to you. However, if they are presented with the plan, which is complete in all respects, their influence will be diminished. They will see that you have given careful thought to all aspects of the family planning process and will realize that you've worked closely with your advisors in creating it. If they don't like the plan, let your advisors shoulder some of the blame.

By allowing family members to participate too soon in the decision-making process, you will permit too many nonbusiness elements to intrude in the formula. It is you who have spent many years, perhaps most of your life, building and nourishing your business. You know it more intimately than any other person in the world. You know best what it will take to continue the business successfully after your departure. And neither your children nor your spouse will have the degree of experience and insight into the intricacies of your business that you have.

As the head of the business, you must lead your family down the proper path of business succession. Certainly you can be flexible when you place your plan before them. Certainly you can listen to their suggestions and ideas. But just as certainly the basic plan must be yours.

All of the above is consistent with my one business maxim: *The operation of successful businesses is more an exercise of enlightened despotism than participatory democracy.* You didn't conduct your business as a democracy; don't decide its future by suddenly introducing that concept now. Your goal is to direct your family to a consensus. So make a good business decision: Prepare your transfer plan and have it ready to be put in place when you present it to the affected parties. Although it can be changed to meet legitimate concerns, you'll have more control.

In short, instead of having to structure a business continuity plan around their sometimes irrational demands, the best possible continuity planning is done before they see it. Even if they have reservations—or don't like it at all—they at least will see a complete plan and learn what you are attempting to do with it. Similarly, nonfamily members who are key employees may well be comforted by the knowledge that when you leave the company there will be a well-conceived plan of business continuity to ensure its viability—and their jobs.

This is another area where outside advisors can be particularly helpful, even essential.

5. Implementing the Plan

Once the decisions have been made, the next step is implementation. This can be accomplished only if proper financial information and legal documentation are prepared in a timely fashion, reviewed, and acted upon. Again, advisors are essential to the process.

Too often I've seen families finally agree on a plan, but fail to follow through with the necessary paperwork and execute the plan. Under those circumstances some family members may conclude that an unsigned plan is no plan at all, while others rely on the oral agreement—all the more reason to put it in writing, sign it, and act upon it.

Now, on to the Cribari family.

I had represented Pat Cribari and his restaurant business for more than ten years. The business had grown steadily through Pat's strenuous efforts, but at the age of 54, he suffered a heart attack. That's when he felt fortunate that he'd earlier brought his eldest son, Anthony, into the business and carefully trained him to assume a management position. Now, Pat thought, he could retire gracefully. After thirty-two years of marriage, he should have known better.

His wife insisted that both of their sons share equally in the business. At the age of 25, the other son, David, was still a junior in college. He was no match for his older brother in competence or ambition. As Pat related this to me, his agitation was clearly evident, and I mentally tried to recall my knowledge of CPR techniques because I was convinced he was about to suffer another seizure.

We examined his situation. Energetic and robust, Pat had not planned on retiring for many years and had done no retirement planning whatsoever. Now he was forced to slow down and entrust the management and operation of the business to others. Since he had little in the way of savings, he would also need to look to the business to provide the bulk of his retirement monies.

With minor variations this is not an atypical situation. Because of the suddenness of his retirement need, several retirement techniques were not available to Pat. But, by calling in his team of advisors—me, an accountant, and a financial planner—he received objective advice on how to proceed.

The financial planner worked with him to identify his specific retirement needs. The accountant determined that the business—if managed properly—could provide sufficient cash flow. Proper management meant that his oldest son, Anthony, must be given the incentive to work harder (and probably more intelligently) than his father had. And it meant putting ownership and control solely in Anthony's hands.

Pat agreed with the advisor team. Now it was time to meet with the other members of the family to obtain a meeting of the minds.

Sure enough, Pat's wife immediately set out to "protect" their youngest son, David, by making certain he got his share. Fortunately we had insisted that *all* family members be present, and it became apparent that David had no interest whatsoever in becoming active in the business. That might mean he'd have to work. When it was suggested to him that instead of receiving his share of the family's estate now in the form of stock, he could be given cash upon his father's death, he quickly saw the wisdom of our plan.

We then explored many different methods of accomplishing Pat's objectives of ensuring sufficient retirement funds while transferring ownership and control to Anthony, and eventually equalizing the estate between Anthony and David. Although we didn't seriously look at all of the following methods of transferring the business, we'll use the Cribari saga to explain the various methods.

Working With Outside Advisors

When a business owner goes through the process of transferring ownership to his child or children, it is usually a new experience. For that reason the owner should call on the services of outside advisors. They are critical to the decision-making process—for a variety of reasons.

One is the experience factor. Unlike the business owner, the properly selected advisor brings to the table his special knowledge and experience gained after years of helping other owners draft and implement transfer plans.

Second, advisors can provide impartiality. This element is often crucial, not only in selecting the best way to transfer the business interest but also in convincing all family members of the correctness of the method. By acting as your representative through all of the preceding steps of the decision-making process, your advisor can serve as a lightning rod—explaining to other family members the reasons for the particular ownership structure that has been decided upon, answering their questions, and defusing any anger that may arise. Thus, by letting your advisors wear the black hats of the "bad guys," you are able to remain the "good guy" in your white hat and retain your relationships with other family members.

This happens because family members are much less likely to question the soundness of decisions if they believe the decisions were made by your advisors rather than you or other family members. For the same reason, outside advisors can also facilitate the decision-making process and the transition of the business to the younger generation by mediating disputes among family members. It is better that they perform this role than you.

Clients often ask, What should good business advisors do? I tell them that business owners, based simply on their experience with their own businesses, may know enough to ask questions 1 through 10. But it is the job of the advisor to ask questions 11 through 50. This means making sure the owner has analyzed all facets of an issue—in this case the decision to transfer ownership of the business to a younger generation.

If your current business accountant or attorney is not experienced in these areas, I strongly suggest you find outside advisors who possess that experience and knowledge for the specific purpose of assisting you in this transaction.

Transferring Ownership Through Stock

The simplest, most common, and often the most effective methods of transferring ownership to children is by *giving* or *selling* them stock. Regardless of the method of transferring ownership to your children, the constant concern is our old friend valuation, a manageable concern when you deal with your children.

One of the great advantages of transferring stock to your children is the absence of arms-length bargaining. In many cases, if you don't have to negotiate with strangers over the price of a stock, you can determine its price based on your retirement needs. However, it is precisely for this reason that the IRS takes such a keen interest in stock transfers between family members.

The IRS is concerned that at an unduly low valuation will

result in a loss to the government of its rightful share of estate taxes. Without arms-length bargaining, the stock could be valued lower than it should, the IRS argues, and for every $1 decrease in value the estate tax loss to the government may be as high as 55 cents on the dollar. Thus, we have a situation where a family wants to value stock as low as possible while the IRS wants it valued as high as possible. Add to this boiling pot of potential litigation the inherent difficulty of valuing stock in a closely held business.

In Chapter 3, we reviewed the Thomas Wells situation, where the Wells family wanted to minimize estate taxes at Thomas Wells's death by transferring as much of the business interest as possible to his children. That's the kind of situation the IRS would examine closely. On the other hand, the fundamental situation with the Cribari family is to value the stock as high as possible to ensure that Pat Cribari can retire on sufficient monies generated from the future earnings of the business. Of these two examples, the IRS would be more concerned about the Wells's situation than Cribari's.

Often these two problems exist side by side. There may be an estate tax concern, yet an overriding concern with satisfying the income needs of the senior generation. Flexibility in valuation and payment techniques can help resolve the difficulties faced by families with an estate tax problem.

Compounding this problem is the fact that the valuation technique used by the family to transfer the stock may be attacked by the IRS years later—at the death of the parent.

So how *is* the value of stock determined in making transfers among family members?

The best solution is to have a third party determine valuation by using a variety of techniques. The third party may be an appraiser or your own certified public accountant. In any case you must avoid a "sweetheart" valuation technique; it must be defendable. By that I mean a neutral party should use recognized valuation methods as described in Chapter 7 to arrive at a valuation that could be defended under oath in a court of law. A lot of this boils down to finding someone to value your business who has experience, credentials, and common sense.

Giving Stock to Offspring

Once the valuation is made, you may decide to transfer the stock by making it a gift to your child or children. Be prepared to pay a gift tax ranging from 34 to 55 percent. Whenever a transfer of property is made for less than fair market value, a gift occurs and a gift tax is imposed on the donor.

There are, however, two primary methods of avoiding this tax. One is the use of the annual *gift tax exclusion*. The exclusion allows $10,000 to be given by each donor to each donee per year. If your spouse participates in your gift, the amount rises to $20,000 ($10,000 from you and $10,000 from your spouse.) Here's how it works: If the stock of your company is worth $200,000, you could transfer 5 percent of the stock worth $10,000 to a child in any given year and no tax would be imposed. If your spouse joined in the gift—even if he or she did not actually own stock—the size of the gift can increase to 10 percent of the stock (worth $20,000). For a spouse to join in a gift, he or she must merely consent to the gift on a gift tax return.

The second way to avoid the tax is by using your *unified credit*. This permits you to give away as much as $600,000 worth of assets during your lifetime to anyone without paying any gift taxes. The major problem this presents is that the unified credit is also used for estate taxes. To the extent you use the unified credit during your lifetime, it's not available upon your death and estate taxes are then due on every dollar of your estate.

The gift and estate tax credits are really just one credit that can be used—either at your death or during your lifetime. Once it's exhausted in your lifetime, it's gone. Nevertheless, it can still make sense to use the unified credit because it removes the appreciation in value of the asset you have given away during your lifetime from taxability at death.

Here's an example: Suppose your company was worth $1 million and you gave away half of it to a daughter who was active in the business. If, at your death, the business has increased in value to $3 million, only $1.5 million—50 percent of the company's worth—would be includable in your estate because you had given away the other half, including the amount of appreciation in that half.

Obviously, the use of the gift tax exclusion and unified credit can be useful in transferring assets now to your children. If you have four children, you could, for example, give each of them $10,000 per year annually ($20,000 if your spouse joins in). The unified credit, however, is yours alone.

The key is to use your annual gift tax exclusion and unified credit in a wise and careful manner as part of an overall plan to transfer your business as well as other assets to your children.

Selling Stock to Offspring

Again, the valuation issue remains critical to the IRS. It is concerned that a parent will sell stock to a child for less than the fair market value, thereby giving away a portion of the stock's value to the child through the "bargain" sale process. And remember, the IRS is concerned with collecting taxes on a gift as well as on a sale.

If, for example, a stock was worth $100 per share and the owner sold it to her child for $30 per share, the gift element would be $70 per share. Consequently, when you sell stock to a child, it's usually necessary to go through the same valuation process as if you had given the stock to the child.

By the way, this entire area of the swamp is one that should be negotiated only with experienced legal and financial counsel serving as navigators. You don't want to overturn in these waters; the bite of the IRS alligator can be most painful as it strikes where you are most sensitive—in your pocketbook.

How to Retain Control and Protect Your Interest

You've made up your mind that you will transfer ownership to a son or daughter. But you're not ready to turn over total control of the company. In fact, you want to make sure you can undo any damage that may result from the transfer.

There are a number of ways to go about this. As a general rule, I suggest you do not transfer voting control to your children until you are ready to give them the entire business. Because of family loyalty (and blindness), it is often tempting to bring children in as owners too early. If you retain control initially, you can see if your decision was well-founded or whether you need to step back in to protect family harmony, not to mention to preserve the business that is probably funding your retirement.

The lesson to be learned is not to give up control until you are absolutely certain you have transferred that power to the right offspring—the one most capable of accepting that responsibility. When that isn't done or isn't done soon enough, your business and your retirement are in jeopardy. Witness what happened to George Rumler.

What happens when your children want to not only run but also control the business before you are sure they are ready? You can sell it to them and take back a note, but you will lose control. Or you can use a technique I call "Oldco/Newco."

Under this planning technique the existing business (Oldco) remains under the parents' control and ownership. A new company, Newco, is formed, owned by the child or children who will run the new business. Oldco leases its equipment, office, warehouse or other facilities, and perhaps even employees to the new company, launching its business. If the new company fails, Oldco and its investment is not at risk; if the new company succeeds, Newco eventually buys the equipment, facilities, and other goodwill from Oldco. This plan worked nicely with Lambert Explosives Manufacturing Company (Lamco).

The owner of Lamco was ready to slow down and turn the business over to his youngest child, Sherry. However, Lambert knew one serious error on her part could figuratively send the business, most of it involving government contract work, up in smoke.

We had Sherry set up a new, woman-owned enterprise. This status gave her an advantage in bidding for government contracts. She successfully obtained contracts and leased the manufacturing facilities and equipment from Lamco at a fair market value rental rate. This enabled Fred Lambert to retire in comfort and security.

Over the years I've used this technique successfully with construction companies, tire distributorships, and other types of companies where capital investment was extensive.

Involving a Third Party

Another technique that helps you avoid family conflict while selling the business to a child involves a third party. The simplest example is to have your child buy your business and finance at least a substantial part of the purchase through a bank.

Your child borrows as much as is feasible—usually no more than half of the purchase price. The bank takes a first lien against all of the equipment, accounts receivable, and inventory (and probably a personal guarantee from you until the loan is reduced to a comfortable level). One of the conditions of the loan will probably be your reinvolvement in the business if a default appears imminent.

Also related to bank financing is a technique by which you sell part of your business to someone in addition to your children. This could be, for example, an ESOP, a group of key employees, or another co-owner who is not a family member. The terms and conditions would be, of necessity, arms length; any subsequent default would be triggered by someone other than yourself. This is precisely what happened with Sidewall Manufacturing Company.

The Sidewall Company, producers of aluminum siding, gutters, and roofing materials, was owned by Claude Reha, who wanted to retire and leave his two children in control of the business. But the value of the business was too high for the sons to buy it or for Claude to give it to them. Also, Claude's intended retirement lifestyle would require a lot of bucks.

The solution was to have Claude sell 45 percent of his stock to a leveraged ESOP for $1 million. The ESOP obtained the money via a bank loan. The bank secured the loan with all of the assets of the company as well as Claude's personal guarantee. Claude then sold 25 percent of the stock to a group of three employees and the remaining 30 percent of his stock to his two children.

Claude gave fairly generous payout terms for the children and key employees—interest only until the bank loan could be retired and then interest and principal over eight years.

One of the conditions of the bank loan required that if the bank felt insecure because of the company's financial position or if the ESOP or company defaulted on the note, Claude would return to the company and resume total control of its operations until the bad financial position or default was cured. This allowed Claude to have a third party—the bank—determine the performance of the new management and ownership, which included his children. It allowed, indeed required, Claude to come back into the business when the company was not satisfying its obligations to its primary creditor—the bank.

This scenario worked beautifully in the actual example. The bank, for justifiable reasons, did become uneasy with the new management's performance, and Claude reentered the business for about nine months. During that period he restructured the business and got it back on the right track. While feelings were somewhat strained, everyone worked together to solve the problem because they all had something at stake and knew exactly what needed to be done.

As a final resort, you can always rely upon well-drafted contracts and buy-and-sell agreements, which give you at least the legal right to come back into the business if a child defaults on his obligation to you. It's at least as important, if not more so, in a family situation than in an arms-length, third-party sale, to have clear, concise contract language so that there are no misunderstandings.

In many situations it may be best not to sell the controlling interests in the business to a child until your death. At this point a buy-and-sell agreement requires the child to buy the remainder of your interest. Insurance on your life that is paid for by your child or by the company can provide your spouse with a full cash buyout. Therefore, he or she need not be concerned with your child's ability to run the company. Until then, you remain in control although your child could be given daily or operational control.

The Repurchase Agreement

Assuming that you do give or sell some stock to a child during your life, to protect you against your misplaced generosity *the business must have a repurchase agreement*. This is nothing more than a specialized form of the buy-and-sell agreement. It's used as a "damage control instrument." Here's how it works:

If your child leaves the business for any reason—whether he quits or is fired—he must sell his stock back to the company or to you for a predetermined price, usually low. This buyback provision is often part of an overall business continuity agreement, which also provides for the complete transfer of your stock upon your death, disability, or retirement.

How to Regain Control

The methods discussed above work well. Typically, children are given or sold stock over a period of time as they assume more and more responsibility in the business while the owner cuts back on his own involvement. A point is normally reached, however, where the offspring are given or sold the balance of the stock, thereby assuming full control. That doesn't mean the owner is helpless—if he's planned properly.

If he still looks to the business for money, either in the form of current or deferred compensation, or for installments due for the sale of his stock, it's critical that he place himself in the position of a well-secured creditor of the company and of the children who now own the business. Unless you can afford to walk away from the money the company should be paying you, you need at least as much in the way of written agreements in dealing with family as you would if you sold to a stranger. Nothing can destroy a family like misunderstandings over money!

One of my clients suffered considerable anguish while learning this lesson. He had reached retirement age and, according to an earlier agreement, sold his stock to his daughter and son-in-law, both of whom worked in the company. He sold the stock at a relatively low value and, in return, was permitted to remain on the payroll at $6,000 per month while he continued to perform services for the company.

Shortly after the stock was transferred, the son-in-law decided the company could not afford to keep a "nonproductive employee." My client was given the choice of "early retirement" or full-time work at 40 percent of his normal pay. He chose instead to sue. The legal battle cost not only money and time, but a family as well, although my client eventually got his company back.

While no method and no amount of planning can transform a rotten son-in-law, adequate legal protection at least can keep him from running roughshod over his benefactor.

The Infamous Section 2036(c)

In late 1987 Congress enacted a new section in the tax code. Labeled 2036(c), this section has been described as a harbinger of "the death of the family business." Perhaps that language is too strong, but it does require business owners to plan even more carefully than prior to its passage.

Section 2036(c) is designed to prevent the transfer of business interests from parents to children where the effect of the transfer is to produce income from the business for the parents while allowing a disproportionate share of future appreciation to pass to the children.

The section doesn't prevent transfers from one generation to the next, but it does mean that those transfers may be ineffective in terms of transferring value out of the older generation's estate to the younger generation. At a parent's death the appreciated value of the property transferred to the children is brought back into the parent's estate for estate tax purposes. Where estate taxes are not a concern, you need not worry about this code section.

That was the case with Pat Cribari, owner of the restaurant we visited earlier. His chief objective was to generate income, not transfer value to a younger generation. It was different, however, for Thomas Wells, owner of the construction company. You'll recall we installed a nonstock incentive program for his key employees. The stock was to remain within the Wells family.

The problem faced by Wells was twofold. The first was to transfer the existing $1.5 million business to his son. Second, to the extent he would be unable to transfer the business, Wells wanted to at least eliminate all future appreciation in value on the business interest he retained while allowing his son's business interest to carry with it all of the future appreciation.

Obviously, it does no good to transfer a business interest to a child for estate planning purposes, only to retain a business interest that grows and appreciates in value and therefore fails to eliminate the estate tax problems.

Summary

The problems facing parents who wish to transfer the business to their children are many. It's worth repeating the five-step process described in this chapter, which can prevent, not just remedy, your own family version of "Dallas." For your convenience, that list is repeated below.

DECISION-MAKING CHECKLIST

☐ 1. Determine how much money you want from your business.
☐ 2. Determine your timetable.
☐ 3. Determine your ownership structure.
☐ 4. Obtain a consensus for your plan.
☐ 5. Implement the plan.

9

Planning for the Unforeseen

The business continuity agreement: the most important document in your business

The business continuity agreement is the single most important document that you, as the owner of a closely held business, will sign. To understand why this is so, we must first review what the business continuity agreement does.

The business continuity agreement (also called a buy-and-sell agreement) controls the transfer of ownership in a business when certain events occur. Typically these events include the death of a shareholder and a sale and transfer of stock from one shareholder to another or to an outside party.

In addition to controlling these events, you should also consider having the agreement include transfers to take effect upon an owner's permanent and total disability, termination of employment, retirement, bankruptcy, divorce, or—importantly—a business dispute among the owners.

At each of these events, the business continuity agreement may require the business or the remaining shareholders to purchase the departing shareholder's stock; or it may give an option to either the business and remaining shareholders to

162

buy that shareholder's stock. Conversely, it may give the departing shareholder the option to require the company to buy his stock. The agreement should also establish the value of the stock, set the terms and conditions of the buyout, and give additional protections to all shareholders.

In short, the business continuity agreement, in addition to other protections, tells you to whom you can sell and what price and terms, and under what restrictions you *can* sell—or *must* sell—your stock. These restrictions will be explored in the rest of this chapter.

Advantages and Disadvantages

Lawyers, being lawyers, are reluctant to discuss the advantages of any action without also discussing the disadvantages. This healthy characteristic helps us keep our clients out of trouble. With buy-and-sell agreements, however, disadvantages are hard to find if the document is well drafted and kept updated for changes in ownership, value, and other circumstances.

With that in mind, let's first look at the advantages.

Advantages

• *Ownership in the business can be transferred only in accordance with the agreement.* This benefits both the owner wishing to transfer stock and the other owner or owners wanting to acquire it. In the first instance, it can assure a selling shareholder, or his estate, of a purchaser for fair value and upon terms and conditions that are mutually acceptable. For the remaining owners the agreement means that any transfers of ownership must be made, or at least offered, to him. This eliminates the threat that an outside party or a co-owner's spouse or children will become owners of the business, thereby diminishing management, control, and value.

• *Valuation is set not only for purposes of a sale but also for estate tax valuation purposes.* Privately owned businesses are notoriously difficult to value. Your idea of your business's value at your death may be much lower than the IRS's. If you haven't fixed the value of your business, the IRS is free to use a variety of valuation techniques in an attempt to maximize value so it can impose the highest estate tax liability on your estate. A properly drafted buy-and-sell agreement can fix that value.

• *The terms and conditions of any transfer of stock, including interest rate, length of buy-out period, and security, can be fixed.* In addition, where possible, the transfer can be funded. The agreement provides a clear picture to a departing shareholder of how much money he will receive, and how often. Likewise, the remaining shareholders know in advance the extent and duration of their buyout obligations. This allows both parties to plan their future.

• *Buy-and-sell agreements establish and protect rights among shareholders that do not otherwise exist in the company.* Through a buy-and-sell agreement, a minority shareholder may attain more control over his or her destiny than is normally provided through voting rights. These safeguards include placing limits on the sale or purchase of the stock of the majority owner(s), establishing valuation for all owners' stock, and other important items.

An example of this is providing the owner of a minority interest the right to serve on the board of directors. Obviously this can be an important right, because a minority shareholder might not otherwise be able to garner sufficient votes to be elected to the board.

In another example the corporation and remaining shareholders can be required to do their best to obtain the release of the departing shareholder from any personally guaranteed indebtedness as well as to release any personal collateral used for a corporate debt when the owner of that collateral sells his interest in the company.

• *An intangible benefit lies in the process of designing the buy-and-sell agreement.* All too often when there are joint owners of a business, they do not sit down together to discuss business issues. In order to draft a buy-and-sell agreement, however, a meeting of all owners is essential. In doing so, they address major questions affecting their relationship such as What happens if one of the owners dies? If they don't get along? If one wants to retire before the other? Obtaining answers to these important questions requires them to discuss their ideas about the future of the business.

I will always remember one of my client companies where the two owners, equal partners, had a poor relationship. They were certain each had opposing views on the future of the business—in terms of both growth and their respective desires to remain in the business. And they each had their own ideas about their own importance to the business.

In meetings with their advisory team, they soon learned there were many reasons for their business's success. Although one owner was the "money man" and the other more active in the business, they learned both were equally concerned with the long-term future of the company. This recognition allowed us to draft a complete buy-and-sell agreement for their mutual benefit.

The process took almost a year. During that time the owners met periodically with their advisors to review business goals and aspirations. Increasingly, they found themselves in agreement—not just in matters contained in the buy-and-sell agreement, but also with respect to operational ideas. Those bases of agreement soon broadened into a consensus on how the business should proceed if one of them were no longer with it.

As a result their business today is more vibrant, more directed. The owners are more committed than ever. And not coincidentally, profitability and value have increased steadily.

• A buy-and-sell agreement *establishes a market for your stock at an agreed-upon price.* Without an agreement there's no market for stock in a closely held business unless you're a controlling owner. Otherwise—if you've not made firm arrangements for the sale of your stock—the buy-and-sell agreement is the only means of disposing of your ownership interest at a fair price. The agreement can then obligate others to purchase your stock, thus creating a market, at an agreed-upon price. It also provides a market if you must sell your stock due to unforeseen events such as death or disability.

As is evident from the above, there are many advantages to a buy-and-sell agreement. But there are also disadvantages. Here are the most common:

Disadvantages

• *Legal fees can be a stumbling block.* An agreement may easily cost $800 to $5,000 or more, although most buy-and-sell agreements that are relatively straightforward, but still comprehensive and thorough, are closer to the low end of this scale.

• *Drafting a complete buy-and-sell agreement is difficult.* It's virtually impossible to anticipate every contingency. This is especially true when the attorney first begins to represent the business. After a while, when the buy-and-sell agreement has been reviewed at several fiscal year-end meetings, revisions will normally occur. As a result the business continuity agreement can be tailored to the particulars of the business.

• *The need to keep the buy-and-sell agreement up to date.* Because a buy-and-sell agreement is a long-term contract, its provisions must be reviewed with your advisors at every fiscal year-end meeting. Like other living organisms, a closely held business continually grows or contracts. The dynamics of ownership, valuation, and events that could trigger a buyout require constant monitoring, updating, and adaptation. The cost in time and money is usually not significant, but the practice must be habitual.

The Typical Buy-and-Sell Agreement

The pattern of a typical business continuity agreement and most important provisions of the agreement are discussed below in the order they would normally appear in buy-and-sell agreements. An outline of the business continuity agreement is included in the Appendix. You may wish to read the relevant provision in the outline before that particular article is discussed.

Mandatory vs. Optional Buyouts

Before looking at the different types of events that could trigger a stock transfer, keep in mind what type of purchase or sale obligation, if any, you want to impose on the transaction.

For example, if a shareholder terminates his employment, the buy-and-sell agreement could require that shareholder to sell—and require his company to buy—his stock. Alternatively, it could also require the company or remaining shareholders to purchase the stock of a departing shareholder only at the option of that shareholder. The buy-and-sell agreement could also give the company or remaining shareholder an option to purchase the stock of a departing shareholder if the company or shareholder chooses to do so.

In addition to showing how each transfer event will obligate the company or remaining or departing shareholders, the obligation decision interacts with valuation and payment issues. For example, if a shareholder is fired, the company may want the option, but not the obligation, to purchase his stock—possibly at a value that is less than the fired shareholder might have received had he worked until retirement.

Who Should Buy?

Yet another consideration in the buy-and-sell agreement is who should buy the selling shareholder's stock—the company or the other owners? This issue is resolved by asking

1. Which entity has the most cash available to pay for the stock? The company or the individual owners?
2. At what level do the most favorable tax consequences occur?

Generally, where the buyout of a departing shareholder's stock is not funded by some form of insurance, the corporation is more likely to have cash available to fund an installment buyout. Also, the tax consequences may not be as severe when the company pays.

Of course, when the remaining shareholder sells his stock during his lifetime, there will generally be taxes to be paid on the amount of gain. The gain can be reduced (especially in a death buyout where insurance funding is available) by having the remaining shareholders purchase the departing shareholder's stock. This is called a cross-purchase buyout. When the corporation buys the selling owner's stock, the situation is called a stock redemption. The substantial tax advantage of a cross-purchase arrangement to the remaining shareholders, when it comes time to sell their stock, is illustrated in the example of George Kilpatrick and Barbara Joy, described in the following section.

Because, as a business owner, you should always be planning for the eventual sale of your business, you cannot afford to ignore this difference between a cross purchase and a redemption.

The Death Buyout

A business continuity agreement almost always contains provisions for the purchase of a shareholder's interest upon his death; but there are certain exceptions to this general principle. One exception occurs when the business interest is strictly investment-oriented.

For example, if the business owner has been a passive investor—receiving large distributions from the business each year—he may want his heirs to continue receiving those distributions after his death. In that instance the agreement can be drafted to allow remaining owners to control the future of the business while the heirs are assured a continued return on their investments.

Another exception occurs when, for estate and personal reasons, it may be appropriate to allow the transfer of a deceased shareholder's interest to family members, rather than to the remaining shareholders. This concept is more fully explored in Chapter 11.

These rare exceptions aside, in most situations a shareholder's death should create an explicit obligation on the part of his estate to sell his stock, either to the corporation or to the remaining shareholders. There should also be an explicit obligation on the part of the corporation or the remaining shareholders to purchase that stock.

The purpose of creating these mandatory obligations is straightforward. Very few owners want to be in business with their co-owner's spouse or children—for obvious reasons. Most closely held businesses require the owners to actively participate in the business enterprise. Few spouses or children can fill the shoes of the deceased owner, and the remaining owner or owners usually are unwilling to continue the effort that's required to make the business successful if much of the benefit will accrue to a passive owner.

In some respects stock ownership means little in a closely held business unless the owner is in a position to use the stock to control his livelihood. A decedent's spouse or children are unlikely to be in that position. Upon his death they are not likely to demand a fair market value for their stock. By requiring the remaining shareholders to purchase his stock, the decedent makes certain that his family will receive the value—hard cash—set forth in the agreement. Without a buy-and-sell agreement, this conversion of what is generally the largest, but most illiquid, asset of the estate may not happen. The advantages of such an agreement are illustrated in the case of George Kilpatrick and Barbara Joy.

The Killjoy Caper

In 1963 George Kilpatrick and Barbara Joy started up a company called—what else?—Killjoy Manufacturing. Each paid $1,000 for one half of the stock, giving each a $1,000 basis in their stock.

George and Barbara came to my company for a buy-and-sell agreement at the suggestion of their insurance agent. Their company was now worth a half million, and the insurance agent wanted it to buy two $250,000 life insurance policies—one on each owner's life. The premium on both policies would total $20,000 per year, about $10,000 for each. The agent explained that the premiums, while not tax-deductible, are more affordable to the corporation because it is in a lower tax bracket than the owners and has more cash available than they have. As already discussed, this type of a buyout—in which the corporation purchases the decedent's stock—is known as a *stock redemption.*

Under this plan, upon George's death the corporation would use the tax-free insurance proceeds to buy his stock, leaving Barbara the sole owner of all the outstanding stock in the business. Her basis remains at $1,000. If, after a period of time, she decides to sell Killjoy to a friendly competitor, a national corporation, or anyone else—and if Killjoy has not appreciated in value—her gain would be $499,000. A tax of $150,000 would be due.

I instead recommended a cross-purchase agreement. Barbara, the surviving shareholder, would purchase George's stock after his death, using $250,000 of income-tax-free proceeds from the insurance that she, not the company, would buy on George's life.

For George's estate the result is the same under either scenario: The estate receives $250,000 income tax free (under the step-up in basis rules explained in Chapter 11).

But for Barbara the results are very different. If the second plan (the cross purchase) is followed, when she sells the stock her gain is only $249,000 and her tax on that gain is only $75,000. To obtain this favorable tax result, all she had to do was buy the stock instead of having the corporation buy it. This meant that she needed to own the insurance policy so that she would receive the life insurance proceeds, income tax free. As the insurance agent pointed out, because of her higher tax rate, it would cost Barbara more to buy the policy than it would the company; however, given the substantial tax savings down the road, it seemed to make sense to have her bear that expense. Fortunately there is a way for Barbara to have the tax benefit of the cross purchase using tax-free insurance proceeds while avoiding, in large part, the tax cost of paying for that insurance. It's called split dollar insurance.

A split dollar insurance agreement divides the ownership and the corresponding premium payments between the corporation and the individual. In Barbara's case the agreement required the corporation to pay about 85 percent of the premium payment on the policy on George's life in return for the right to receive the cash value buildup in the policy. Thus, at George's death, the business would receive essentially a return of all the premium payments and Barbara would receive the remaining death proceeds.

The reason for the split dollar insurance agreement is to make certain that the bulk of the income tax consequences on the payment of the insurance premium remain at the corporate level. Yet the insurance proceeds could be payable to Barbara to allow her to get an increased basis in the company upon George's death.

These examples show the importance of a coordinated planning approach to your business. Through proper planning an income tax savings of $75,000 was created without any inconvenience, complications, or disadvantage to anyone—except, perhaps, the IRS.

I often review a buy-and-sell agreement for a new client only to find that the valuation for death purposes is unrealistically high. Invariably this happens because it's easy to buy a lot of life insurance to fund the purchase of the decedent's stock—a mistake that can lead to serious consequences.

Unfortunately, most buy-and-sell agreements are not reviewed often enough. Sometimes the underlying life insurance policies lapse and the owner subsequently dies, leaving no insurance owned by the corporation or other shareholders. In that situation the underlying obligation remains—to purchase at an inflated value while there's no funding available. And when the valuation is large—several hundred thousand dollars or more for a decedent's stock—overvaluing the stock may lead to estate taxes that are otherwise avoidable.

In short, overvaluing for death purposes is just plain sloppy. It happens because the owner reasons, "Well, life insurance is cheap, and it doesn't really make a difference how much my company is worth. If I die, my wife will get the money." All this does is allow the business owner to avoid the critical thinking so necessary to determine the true value of his business. And until he determines that true value, how can he expect to measure increases in that value?

The issues surrounding valuation, including methods of

properly valuing your business, are discussed in detail in Chapter 7. For purposes of this context, the point is simply this:

The same effort to arrive at a fair value for your business interest must be made for buy-and-sell purposes. In addition to events that can be funded with insurance, such as death and disability, the buy-and-sell agreement normally includes events where funding is not available: involuntary transfers, business dispute buyouts, sales to third parties, and retirement or termination of employment.

In these cases an accurate value can be even more critical, because the company will have to fund the buyout purely out of cash flow. If the value is too high or the terms too severe, these buyouts can destroy the company.

When Disability Strikes

Most closely held business owners are active in their business. Should they become disabled, the company will endure substantial hardships, both economically and in operations. More importantly, in the absence of a buy-and-sell agreement, the disabled owner's income stream from the company may also evaporate. This problem confronted Steve Hughes, one of three equal shareholders in a growing advertising agency.

At age 38, Steve suddenly had a stroke. As with many stroke victims, his recovery was incomplete. Physically he was the picture of health; but he totally lost his ability to speak and read. Doctors told him he would never be able to return to work.

Hughes's firm had a buy-and-sell agreement, but it covered only a buyout at death and an option for the company to buy his stock if he were to try to sell it to a third party. Trying to find and sell closely held stock to a third party is a difficult proposition anytime; his disability made it impossible. Even if his fellow shareholders had wanted to continue his salary, they did not have the resources to do so indefinitely.

As a result the company and Hughes were left in a classic dilemma: the company—the remaining shareholders—wanted to purchase Hughes's stock so that its future appreciation in value, due now to their efforts alone, would be fully available to them. Conversely, as Hughes's family soon realized, the owners of closely held stock rarely receive current benefits in the form of dividends. The profits of a closely held corporation are either accumulated by the company or distributed to the active shareholders in the form of salaries, bonuses, and other perks.

In short, Hughes's family would not get what they need most—cash—to replace the salary he was no longer earning, while his partners faced the prospect that their efforts to increase the value of the business would reward Hughes as much as themselves. This dilemma could be solved only by a buyout of Hughes's stock. Then his family could receive a fair value for his business interest where they otherwise would receive nothing until the company was eventually sold or liquidated. Meanwhile, ownership would be left with those responsible for the company's success.

The Hughes buyout faced three difficult problems, each of which could have been eliminated by a properly drawn and funded buy-and-sell agreement that would

1. Agree upon the value.
2. Fund the buyout.
3. Agree on the payment terms of the buyout.

The disability of a key owner may, and probably will, reduce revenue (at least for awhile) and increase expenses because of the need to hire replacement personnel. However, if properly planned, the company can prepare to pay that fair value by purchasing disability buyout insurance. The buy-and-sell agreement, in combination with the disability buyout policy, provides the means to achieve both the disabled shareholder's goal of receiving money for his ownership interest, and the company and remaining shareholders' goals of maintaining active ownership.

Don't confuse the terms *disability buyout insurance* and *disability income replacement insurance*. The latter, discussed in Chapter 10, can help replace lost income in the event of disability. The insurance company normally pays a percentage of the disabled owner's regular monthly salary directly to him until he overcomes his disability or attains a certain age, such as 65. *Disability buyout insurance* is paid to the business in a lump sum or series of payments over several years. The company then pays that money to the disabled owner to buy back his stock. Disability buyout insurance intended to fund a buy-and-sell agreement should be acquired in addition to the owner's personal disability income insurance.

The buy-and-sell agreement also addresses payment terms. Since disability buyout insurance will normally not cover more than 80 percent of the buyout price, a "balance owing" usually results. This means the owner and shareholders must agree on the payment terms for the remaining amount owed. Typically these terms are the interest rate, the length of the buyout period (usually three to seven years), and the security to be given to ensure payment for the balance owing.

When these key elements are negotiated in advance— before any of the shareholders become disabled—fair and equitable decisions can be made. In the Steve Hughes case, it was too late. His family eventually felt compelled to sell his stock for book value—a low return for a service company. It was that or nothing. Besides, it was all that his former partners felt they could afford to pay.

Other Events

So far we've covered the primary events—death and disability—that trigger a transfer of ownership. The buy-and-sell agreement should also cover other types of involuntary or court-ordered transfers such as a shareholder's bankruptcy or divorce. In either event the shareholder could be forced to transfer his ownership interest—in the case of bankruptcy, to the bankruptcy trustee or creditor; in the case of divorce, to the former spouse.

The buy-and-sell agreement should simply give the business the opportunity to acquire the shareholder's stock in the event of an involuntary transfer. Perhaps the only thing worse than having your ex-spouse own a part of your business is having someone else's ex-spouse own a part of your business! As Jimmy Durante would say, "What a revolting development this is!"

In addition to those involuntary transfers—death, disability, bankruptcy, divorce—a well-drafted business continuity agreement should also cover events generally within the control of one or more of the shareholders. Where there are two equal owners, one of whom is president, an agreement can provide that the president can't fire the other owner. And where there are three equal shareholders, two of them would generally have the power to fire the third.

In that event they might want the ability to purchase the terminated owner's stock. The fired owner may want the ability to sell his stock back to the company. Or all the owners may simply want the agreement to require a mandatory purchase of stock in the event of a termination of employment of a shareholder for any reason, whether he quits or is fired.

Again, when this situation occurs—as it often does—the scene is acrimonious and hostile. Litigation is always threatened or initiated. This is when a buy-and-sell agreement—one that has determined a fair market value for the business and the terms and conditions and has been agreed upon by all parties—can truly be a godsend.

Third-Party Offers

Every buy-and-sell agreement should cover restrictions on transferring stock to nonowners. Without this provision the agreement is toothless; an owner would be able to transfer his stock to anyone, at any time, thereby avoiding the agreement's other provisions.

If an ownership interest is to be offered to an outsider, the agreement normally requires the owner to first offer his interest to the company, then to the remaining co-owners—at the same price and terms offered by the would-be buyer.

My agreements usually require that the purchase price offered the remaining owners be the lower of the value set forth in the agreement or the price offered by the would-be purchaser. This assures the remaining owners that they need pay no more than the value fixed in the agreement.

"The Texas Shootout" Provision

When there are two or more noncontrolling owners, neither may be able to fire or get rid of the other(s) in the absence of a provision in the buy-and-sell agreement. Similarly, because the president of the company may be able to terminate other equal shareholders, the agreement may preserve the employment of all the owners.

It is when owners are locked in a bitter dispute with respect to the future course of the business enterprise that the buy-and-sell agreement can become most valuable. It can become the means to resolve the dispute by forcing one or more disgruntled owners to sell their stock and get out of the business.

The agreement may stipulate that any shareholder may make an offer to purchase the other shareholder's interest. The second shareholder must then either accept the offer and sell his stock or purchase the first owner's interest for the same price, terms, and conditions spelled out in the offer. In other words the second shareholder has two choices: He must either accept the offer and sell his stock or turn the tables and buy the offering shareholder's stock.

At the conclusion of this buyout procedure, there will be only one shareholder. I call this method the Texas shoot-out provision. It's a painful remedy undertaken only when there is no alternative that the parties can agree on. I like to have this provision in a buy-and-sell agreement; it tends to encourage owners who are not getting along with each other to agree to a buyout of one party or the other. If they don't, the foot-dragging partner cannot prevent the eventual buyout of his stock.

The buy-and-sell agreement could provide one other alternative. It could allow either party—if both parties can't get along—to dissolve the corporation, pay off the debts, distribute the assets, and start all over.

The Sole Owner

The buy-and-sell agreement can be even more important for a sole owner. Should you die or become totally disabled, there is no natural "market" to sell your stock to. This can be especially critical in personal service companies where there is little value other than the "going concern value" (as discussed in Chapter 7). But don't despair. Business continuity agreements can be designed for situations where there is only one owner.

In this situation it's necessary to locate another owner of a business, usually similar to yours, who would also like to provide some type of continuity for his or her business. For example, I've prepared agreements for a group of independently practicing oral surgeons. If one of them should die, become disabled, or retire, the remaining surgeons have the obligation to purchase the departing surgeon's practice.

In a case of sole business owners, I've also drafted in their buy-and-sell agreements a total, temporary disability provision that requires the other parties of the agreement to help maintain the business or practice of the temporarily disabled individual until he recovers. If the sole owner is a surgeon, for example, who suffered a broken hand, the other surgeons must cover his practice and work a specified number of hours a week at a specified rate of pay. This is cheap insurance, indeed, to protect and preserve the value of the disabled surgeon's practice.

In lieu of finding another business to be a party to the buy-and-sell agreement, you'll need to turn to your key employees. This type of buyout provides a good incentive to such employees, since they know you have committed to ultimately selling the business to them, either at your retirement, disability, or death.

Summary

The buy-and-sell agreement should cover certain events that trigger a transfer of stock—death, disability, involuntary transfer, termination of employment, and irreconcilable business disputes.

The agreement should also cover the terms and conditions of a buyout that is not totally funded by some form of insurance—the term of the buyout, the interest rate on the unpaid balance, and the security to be given to the selling shareholder.

These provisions might be different for each event. For example, since most death buyouts are at least partially funded by life insurance, the unpaid balance is likely to be much smaller and thus paid off in a shorter time frame than in the case of the unfunded lifetime transfer.

As you can see, there are literally hundreds of decisions that must be made in the buy-and-sell agreement. All these decisions may seem legalistic and overly technical. But I can assure you that should an event causing a stock transfer arise, the decisions you make now will be the most important "minutia" your business deals with.

A buy-and-sell agreement is the most important business document you will ever create. It is a mechanism that maintains control over the business by the active shareholders. For the departing shareholder, it guarantees a fair value, a ready market for his stock, and equitable terms and conditions of any buyout of his stock. No other document will do this.

To help you design your own buy-and-sell agreement, the following checklist highlights seven events that could trigger a transfer of stock under a buy-and-sell agreement. It's unlikely your buy-and-sell agreement will need to include all, or even most, of these events. However, I've provided a variety of issues that must be addressed under each event. You must familiarize yourself with these issues and make a number of decisions.

CHECKLIST: EVENTS THAT COULD TRIGGER A STOCK TRANSFER UNDER A BUY-AND-SELL AGREEMENT

☐   I. Death.

      A. Buyout (select one).

          1. Mandatory purchase and mandatory sale.

      2. Optional purchase to business or remaining share-
        holders.

    B. Terms and Conditions.

      1. Percentage of down payment.
      2. Length of installment note.
      3. Interest rate of installment note.

☐ II. Disability.

    A. Buyout (select one).

      1. Mandatory.
      2. Optional to business or remaining shareholders.
      3. Optional to disabled shareholder (or selling share-
        holder).

    B. Terms and Conditions.

      1. Percentage of down payment.
      2. Length of installment note.
      3. Interest rate of installment note.

☐ III. Transfer to Third Party.

    A. Buyout (select one).

      1. Mandatory.
      2. Optional to business or remaining shareholders.

    B. Terms and Conditions.

      1. Percentage of down payment.
      2. Length of installment note.
      3. Interest rate of installment note.
      4. Price to be paid: price offered or value stated in
        agreement?

☐ IV. Termination of Employment.

    A. Buyout (select one).

      1. Mandatory.

   2. Optional to business or remaining shareholders.
   3. Optional to terminating employee/shareholder.

  B. Terms and Conditions.

   1. Percentage of down payment.
   2. Length of installment note.
   3. Interest rate of installment note.
   4. Price.

☐ V. Retirement.

  A. Buyout (select one).

   1. Mandatory.
   2. Optional to business or remaining shareholders.
   3. Optional to deceased retiring shareholder.

  B. Terms and Conditions.

   1. Percentage of down payment.
   2. Length of installment note.
   3. Interest rate of installment note.
   4. Price.

☐ VI. Involuntary Transfer Due to Bankruptcy or Divorce.

  A. Buyout (select one).

   1. Mandatory.
   2. Optional to business or remaining shareholders.

  B. Terms and Conditions.

   1. Percentage of down payment.
   2. Length of installment note.
   3. Interest rate of installment note.
   4. Price.

☐ VII. Business Disputes.

    A. Buyout (select one).

        1. Mandatory—the Texas Shootout.
        2. Option to sell or liquidate by any shareholder.

    B. Terms and Conditions.

        1. Percentage of down payment.
        2. Length of installment note.
        3. Interest rate of installment note.
        4. Covenants not to compete.
        5. Price.

Part III

Planning for the Owner at the Individual Level

Until now I've emphasized ways to help you plan your business so that you will be able to leave it under the most favorable circumstances. It is the *business itself* that has garnered all our attention. Now it's time to look at the ways in which you can use your business to attain your personal financial goals. By paying careful attention to your personal financial planning and estate planning, you'll be able to keep in check Uncle Sam's influence on your retirement objectives, enabling you to retire comfortably.

10

Meeting Uncle Sam on a Level Paying Field

Financial and personal tax planning for the business owner

As a business owner, you have a need for personal financial planning. You have certain financial goals, but like most people, you're unsure how to go about achieving them. The time and energy you spend starting up and running a successful business or professional practice probably prevents you from giving this subject the thought and planning it requires. Moreover, your business may provide you with many of the rewards you seek while you are active in the business, so you tend to ignore what it can do for you when you leave it.

In Chapter 1 I suggest that you look at a different definition of success in business—one that measures success in terms of the benefits your business will provide when you leave it. One of those benefits is the attainment of your financial goals. That's why a financial plan is so important.

Exactly what is personal financial planning?

G. Victor Hallman and Jerry S. Rosenbloom, both professors at the Wharton School at the University of Pennsylvania, offer this description in their book, *Personal Financial Planning:**

> Personal financial planning is the development of total, coordinated plans for the achievement of one's overall financial objectives. The essential elements of this concept are the development of *coordinated* plans for a person's *overall financial affairs* based upon his or her *total financial objectives.*

Hallman and Rosenbloom believe that although each person's financial objectives may be different depending on his or her individual circumstances, goals, and attitudes, most people seek the following:

- Protection against such personal risks as premature death, disability, and medical expenses.
- Capital accumulation for family, emergencies, and general investments.
- Provision for retirement income.
- Reduction of the tax burden.
- Planning for their heirs.
- Investment and property management.

To develop a plan that will help you attain these objectives, you need the help of specialists. Your advisory team, consisting of an attorney, an accountant, and a financial planner, should provide you with the expertise that is required. Just what is a financial planner, and exactly what does he do?

Despite what you may have heard or read, there's nothing mystical about financial planning or planners. Their general mission is quite simple: to analyze your current financial status and provide recommendations that will help you achieve your financial objectives.

For the average client, the financial planner develops a comprehensive plan that includes five elements: risk manage-

*New York: McGraw-Hill, 1987, pp. 3–5.

ment, investments, tax planning and management, retirement planning and employee benefits, and estate planning. To create such a document, your planner undertakes an analysis of your current financial status, including assets, liabilities, net worth, cash flow, tax projections, insurance plans, employee benefits, risk tolerance, and current investments. Your planner also sits down with you to discuss your intended life-style. Will you cut back on your expenses or continue your spending habits? Do you plan to retire to a poolside in Scottsdale or travel to Sri Lanka and elsewhere?

The business owner has even more specific needs. As an owner you want to get money from the business to your personally. Depending on your goals, needs, and preferences, the financial planner—working with your attorney and accountant—will show you how to minimize your taxes, maximize your investment returns, ensure adequate insurance coverage, and develop a retirement or estate plan.

This plan becomes the link whereby you *integrate your fundamental business objectives with your personal financial and estate planning objectives.* Sound familiar? I list this in Chapter 1 as the third of three key objectives every business owner must focus on.

In Chapter 1 I also say that most business owners look to their business for the bulk of their assets. They need to find a way to use these assets to meet their own financial needs and those of their family. As part of your advisory team, the financial planner will help formulate a plan to do this.

One of the benefits of having a financial planner on your team—this applies to all your advisors—is the opportunity it provides to obtain fresh, objective insights into your business planning. Business owners are frequently an isolated bunch. Caught up in the press of day-to-day crises, they begin to lose perspective. Often they have no firm idea of new planning developments that may affect them—until it's too late to do anything about it. Your financial planner can bring to the table knowledge and experience you don't have. When complemented by the knowledge and experience of your accountant and attorney, his or her input provides you with a formidable array of services and support.

Although financial planners provide comprehensive plans for anyone with income and expenses, the needs of a business owner are more complex. Consequently, your planner will pay special attention to your tax situation, your insurance coverage, and your retirement income needs.

How a Financial Planner Works

Typically a planner follows these steps:

1. Lists your assets, liabilities, projected income, and other information needed to prepare your net worth statement. This is necessary for organizing and defining your current financial situation.
2. Clarifies the timing and financial requirements for your objectives.
3. Examines ways to improve the performance of your financial resources.
4. Identifies and coordinates selected financial services and products needed to make your plan operational.
5. Works with you to implement the plan.
6. Monitors the plan periodically and suggests adjustments when necessary.

Your planner will make recommendations based on projections, analyses, and summaries that reflect your financial resources and objectives. She'll consider such personal factors as age, income, household size, investment experience, and tolerance to risk. Her advice is based on assumptions involving inflation, investment yields, time horizons, tax laws, and economic conditions. Because changes may occur in your personal situation and in these assumptions, you and your planner must be prepared to make periodic adjustments to your plan. This is usually best done in conjunction with your fiscal year-end meeting so that you can benefit from the interplay of all your advisors.

Whenever I discuss financial planning, I immediately recall one of my clients, a senior partner in a heart surgery practice.

The Case of the Spendthrift Surgeon

Dr. Harold Avery appeared to have everything going for him. Because his practice was eminently successful and widely respected, he and his wife enjoyed an enviable life-style. They lived in the most fashionable area of town, and each drove a new Mercedes Benz. When their youngest child had just been graduated from college and was planning to attend graduate school the next year, Dr. Avery came to me with a simple request. He felt it was time to complete a task he had neglected—to draw up a will.

Long ago I had stopped being surprised by the number of business owners who had failed to prepare a will. Incredibly, more than half of them die *intestate*—without a will. In Dr. Avery's case, this problem was irrelevant. I soon discovered he had a more pressing problem:

The good doctor was sixty-three years old—and he was broke!

I couldn't help but compare Dr. Avery's situation with that of another physician client, Dr. Felton (see Chapter 4). Dr. Felton had already contributed enough money to his retirement plan at age 38 so that the requirements of his planned retirement at 59½ were already met. Felton's biggest "problem" was adjusting his plan so that he could retire at age 50 if he chose to do so.

In contrast, here was Dr. Avery at age 63—with no retirement in sight!

I've purposely selected physicians in discussing the role of financial planning for business owners, because physicians traditionally have needed to look to personal financial accumulation planning for their income needs, rather than to the proceeds of a sale of their practice.

Let's use Drs. Avery and Felton to see how each approached their decision making and how you can profit from their experiences. The reason for the different financial outlook between them is, in a word, planning—financial planning, to be precise.

Despite a long and successful practice, Dr. Avery had done no financial planning. He had retained financial planners only to buy the year's hottest tax shelter—an investment that frequently backfired, produced no economic benefit, and was usually challenged by the IRS.

Dr. Avery was a victim of the "TMSTF" syndrome—too-much-success-too-fast. The money had come so easily that he'd succumbed to the temptation of conspicuous spending and life-style. Some business owners can handle this nicely; others fail because they think they've tapped an inexhaustable vein of gold and they don't establish adequate reserves.

The best way to avoid the trap of taking excessive cash out of the business to "live it up" is to create a plan that forces the business owner to confront his needs—now and in his retirement.

That's why Dr. Felton did. In fact, he started using a financial planner when he started his practice. The planner, in turn, introduced him to a good CPA and an adequate business attorney—me. As a team we concentrated on these areas of his financial planning: income tax, investments, fringe benefits, business continuity, and estate conservation.

We approached Dr. Felton's plan as a process that included five steps or phases: (1) determining objectives, (2) making assumptions, (3) evaluating his current situation, (4) making observations, and (5) making recommendations. In so doing we adjusted his plan to allow for his retirement at age 50.

Determining Objectives

Planning is a process that must have goals as an end. These goals, or objectives, are both short- and long-term. They are never to be viewed as immutable; rather, you must review and adjust them continually in the presence of your advisors as part of a full-fledged, joint planning effort.

We divided Dr. Felton's objectives into three categories—*living, disability, and death.*

1. His *living* objectives included the desire to expand and increase the profitability of his practice so that he could bring in a second physician as an employee and eventually establish a group practice. This would enable him to sell his interest when he reached his projected retirement at age 50.

He also wanted to minimize his income taxes, provide for a college education for all three of his children (at an estimated cost of $10,000 a year each for four years), ensure a retirement income of $75,000 per year after taxes beginning at age 50, and find more time for his hobby of glider flying.

2. Next we looked at the *disability* category. The problem there was simply a matter of providing income protection, amounting to $8,000 per month, in the event he became disabled.

3. Finally, we reviewed the *death* category. We identified these objectives: to distribute his assets according to his desires with the least amount of tax and expenses, to provide for a transfer of his practice to his future partners, to provide an education for his children in the event of his death, and to provide income for his wife and children in the amount of $60,000 per year as long as his wife lived.

Making Assumptions

In order to arrive at the objectives, we made certain assumptions. We calculated the anticipated rate of return on investments, the inflation rate for future years, and the ability of the local economy to remain sufficiently strong to allow Dr. Felton's practice to continue to grow. And we assumed that increased regulation of medicine, HMOs, and other methods of reducing health care costs would not, in the long run, be detrimental to his practice.

Evaluating the Current Situation

We examined Dr. Felton's current situation. The financial planner gathered Dr. Felton's income tax returns of the previous four years, financial statements of his business, existing estate planning documents, and insurance policies.

Making Observations

The financial planner noted that Dr. Felton lacked an estate plan and a business continuity plan. He also commented on the amount and type of disability, health, life, and casualty insurance and offered an opinion on whether Dr. Felton's current situation was consistent with his short- and long-term goals.

Making Recommendations

At the fiscal year-end meeting, we first considered the recommendations from the financial planner. Then the CPA and I submitted our own suggestions. Among other planning decisions, our joint efforts produced an estate plan design, a commitment to install and fully fund qualified retirement plans, and a business continuity agreement with a fellow sole practitioner. And those were just the first steps, the initial fruit of an enjoyable relationship that continues today.

Do what we did: Perform these five steps of the financial planning process faithfully, diligently, and with the guidance and support of your advisory team, and you will avoid Dr. Avery's predicament.

Let's look at the financial planning areas we identified earlier.

• *Income Taxes.* Despite recent changes in the tax code, the ability to defer taxes makes the qualified retirement plan the most viable way to create wealth in your business. Many business owners believe they should have only a defined contribution or a profit-sharing plan because they are "flexible" while other types of retirement plans require contributions even if the owner can't afford them. Consequently some owners will take a flyer on risky, tax-oriented schemes upon reaching the funding limit of the defined contribution plan.

Owners have better options than that. A good financial planner will recommend any strategy that allows rapid funding of the plan. Usually, a defined benefit plan will allow more rapid funding for business owners in their fifties. Sometimes this can produce surprisingly high contributions and is tailor-made for owners who suddenly become successful in their late years.

A frequently overlooked plan feature is the $10,000 minimum pension benefit for a spouse who works part-time in the business. This will produce more retirement savings for the family when the owner is at the contribution maximum.

• *Business Continuity.* Because the issue of business succession can be highly emotional, especially for the older business owner, it's often postponed until the last possible moment. That raises serious problems because ownership transfers are most effective when the seller can participate. This is especially true for service businesses and other companies where goodwill is associated with the personality of the owner. Goodwill transfers are hard to do if the owner has already died, become disabled, or retired.

Planning for the succession of your business should begin as early as possible. Ask your financial planner to introduce you to a former business owner, preferably one in your field, who has gone through the experience. Ask that former owner about the problems he faced when planning the succession process. This should encourage you to act now rather than procrastinate any longer.

Estate Preservation and Planning

A key function of the financial planner is to make sure the business owner fully understands the urgency of obtaining insurance protection against the many forces that put his estate at risk. These forces arise in such key areas as business continuation, disability continuation, key-person insurance, business overhead expense, property and liability insurance, and directors' and officers' insurance.

Let's review the need for insurance in each of these areas.

• *Business Continuation.* By definition, a closely held corporation has no open and liquid market for its shares. Yet owners need to know that their share can be transferred at their death. Those shares may have substantial dollar value, but often funds are not available to the surviving owners to buy the shares from the deceased's estate.

One good way to provide such funds is through life insurance. Such policies would insure each business owner with death benefits payable to those who intend to buy the shares from the estate—either the corporation itself or individual owners of the corporation.

• *Disability Continuation.* Long-term disability of a business owner poses an even greater threat to a business than does the owner's death, because the odds of becoming disabled are greater than dying. Therefore, as with death, your financial planner will probably suggest that there should be a disability buyout provision in the buy-and-sell agreement.

There is disability insurance available to help fund disability buyouts. Such policies offer a lump-sum payment or series of payments when a disability occurs, but the buy-and-sell agreement must match exactly the provisions of the disability coverage in terms of the disability's definition and duration. While these policies may have been difficult to obtain in the past, today they are commonplace.

• *Key-Person Insurance.* When a key employee becomes disabled or dies, the consequences to the business could be drastic, especially as it affects revenues. Life insurance policies and disability income policies provide financial protection by enabling the owner to use the benefit payment in a number of ways. It can be used to search for and hire replacements, for general expenditures to compensate for the loss of skills, or to simply shore up the company's financial position.

The corporation generally owns the policies and pays the premiums on the coverage. While the benefits received are generally income tax free, no income tax deduction is allowable for the premium payments.

• *Business Overhead Expense.* Where a business consists of one or two professionals—for example, a physician or accountant who generate all the revenues, unique disability problems exist. If the professional becomes disabled, he may wish to keep his or her office open. This means keeping the office staff on the job. There will be ongoing expenses, even though revenues will be temporarily cut off.

There are policies available to help pay these expenses. Again, the important elements are the definition of disability and the waiting period before the benefits are payable. Benefit payments are usually made for no more than one or two years. That will allow enough time to plan to close or sell off the operation should the disability be permanent.

• *Property Insurance.* Perhaps one of the most important functions a financial planner can serve is to make sure that your property coverage is current and comprehensive. Often an analysis will reveal policies in force on property previously disposed of, or the lack of coverage on newly acquired properties.

Equally important is an evaluation of the amount of coverage. Your financial planner will look at it from two viewpoints: (1) the actual cash value of the property, or what it will yield if sold as used equipment in the marketplace, and (2) its replacement value. Obtaining replacement cost coverage may be appropriate when the difference between the actual cash value of the property and its replacement cost is significant. A professional property insurance agent may be required to search the specialty markets for this kind of coverage.

• *Liability Insurance.* In our "I'll-see-you-in-court" society, all business activity is subject to increasing liability risk. And with multimillion-dollar settlements becoming more common, coverage in some industries is no longer available. Especially vulnerable are those operations where bodily injury incidents run higher than normal. We are all familiar with the difficulties physicians now have in obtaining malpractice insurance. When they do find companies willing to insure them, the premiums may reach astronomical numbers—$30,000 to $100,000 per year!

The liability insurance industry has in recent years been moving to a *claims-made* coverage. This is a policy that provides protection only for those claims filed during the period of coverage. The distinction is important since it doesn't provide coverage for claims made after the period expires even if the incident happened during the period. Your financial planner should help explain it and recommend the coverage you need.

• *Directors' and Officers' Insurance.* These policies should be considered where corporate indemnification is legally or practically unavailable. Designed to protect directors and officers, such policies don't cover deliberate wrongdoing, willful misconduct, or transactions from which the director has obtained personal benefit.

Investment Strategies

Most business owners' assets are tied up in their business and, in many cases, the owner reinvests most or all of his or her profits back into the business. When the business is successful and growing, this is an unbeatable strategy for accumulating wealth. However, there is always the danger the business could face a serious downturn for any number of reasons. To anticipate and offset that possibility, try to invest some of your profits in vehicles outside your own business.

Your financial planner can help you develop and implement the investment strategy. The form of this strategy will be shaped by several factors—the amount of money available, your age, your investment objectives, and your tolerance for risk.

If you are a young business owner whose most productive years are still ahead, your planner may recommend an aggressive program designed to maximize your return. Of course, you may have to invest in such high-risk products as futures and options, penny stocks and speculative stocks, very low-grade bonds, commodities, gold, and collectibles as well as short-term selling.

This strategy can earn you lots of money—if everything goes according to plan. If not, you run the risk of losing significant portions of your investment, perhaps all of it. But, if you are young and healthy and willing to work hard, you have many years ahead to overcome those losses. The question is, Are you psychologically capable of sustaining such losses?

If the answer is no, take a more conservative approach, one that draws you to such vehicles as Series EE government bonds, treasury bills, certificates of deposit, and cash-value life insurance policies. A planner will caution you, however, that to offset the effects of inflation you will want to balance these investments with some reputable, high-quality stocks or real estate investments.

A middle-of-the road approach may see you investing in no-leveraged, or low-leveraged, limited partnerships, common stocks, medium-grade corporate bonds, or investment trusts.

Another major factor in your investment strategy involves the concept of time. Generally, the longer you remain in an investment the less risky it becomes. A diversified stock fund is a good example.

Whatever your risk tolerance is, however, your planner will most likely advise you to adapt a risk-reducing strategy by diversifying. That means investing at least some of your business profits in nonbusiness-related vehicles and ensuring that those investments are also diversified.

Picking a Financial Planner

You should have no trouble attracting the financial planner who's right for you, because financial planners covet having business owners as clients. And why not? Financial planners consider small-business owners to be good clients; they've learned important lessons about life and have realistic expectations of the planner's work. Most owners don't expect their planners to perform miracles. They understand uncertainties, are appreciative when good work is done, and are willing to pay for it. Moreover, they are willing to become long-term clients.

Since financial planners perceive you so favorably, you should have no trouble assembling a list of candidates. So how do you go about selecting one?

The College for Financial Planning,* one of the industry's leading educational institutions, offers these guidelines:

1. Ask your attorney or accountant; referrals are an excellent source. Also ask friends and business associates for recommendations. Then interview at least three candidates.

2. Check the practitioner's academic background. Look for a degree in economics, business administration, or finance and completion of a professional financial planning educational program indicated by such designations as CFP (Certified Financial Planner) or ChFC (Chartered Financial Consultant) as well as evidence of continuing education.

3. Check the candidate's professional experience. Those who have worked in accounting, banking, insurance, or law have the technical background required to offer solid financial planning advice.

4. Request and examine copies of written plans the candidate has completed for other clients. A sound plan should include consideration of risk management, investments, tax planning and management, retirement planning and employee benefits, and estate planning.

5. Ask for client references and the names of other professional advisors with whom the planner may work. Responsi-

*Choosing the Right Financial Planner: A Step-by-Step Guide (Denver: College for Financial Planning, 1987).

ble planners will consult regularly with other professionals who are experts on specific subjects.

6. Determine how the planner is compensated for his or her services. Let's take a closer look at this item.

All financial planners are compensated in one of three ways:

   a. Some are "fee only" planners who may charge a flat fee or by the hour.
   b. Others earn commissions on products sold during plan implementation.
   c. Many charge a combination of fees and commissions. In fact, a study conducted for the College for Financial Planning* showed that the majority derive their income from a combination of fees and commissions on investment products they sell to their clients.

The smallest group of planners are "fee only" planners—those who simply charge a fee to develop a comprehensive plan. Their fee is usually scaled to the client's net worth and the complexity of the plan; they sell no investment products.

The idea of financial planners selling investment products is a subject of ongoing debate within the industry. Fee-only planners believe they are more objective in providing professional advice because they are not motivated, either consciously or otherwise, by the need to earn commissions. They advise clients to adopt certain investment strategies without recommending specific products, such as bond or stock funds, real estate investment trusts, commodities, collectibles, or other vehicles. Their clients are free to buy such products anywhere they choose.

Commission-based planners reply that their clients have no problem with the format. "If I can steer my client toward a nice return on his investment, he's not bothered by the fact I

*Trends in Financial Planning (Denver: College for Financial Planning, 1988).

made a few dollars on the product," a planner recently told me.

Planners who do receive commissions should be willing to reveal how much they earn on the products they recommend. And they should also offer the client a choice of products instead of pushing one over others.

The right compensation method is the one (or two) that makes you comfortable and that provides the financial planner with the incentive to do the best job for you.

I would add that the financial planner you select must be an excellent team player. He or she must be able to engage in the important give-and-take sessions with your other advisors—the attorney and accountant. There must be good chemistry among all three.

Another word of caution when selecting your financial planner: Because of the lack of regulation and standardized credentialing, it's been easy for people to hang out a shingle and call themselves a "financial planner." An estimated 250,000 people have done so. Reports of clients losing their life's savings to unscrupulous "planners" fill the columns of newspapers and the files of state attorneys general and the Securities and Exchange Commission.

However, while the scam artist and fly-by-night practitioner gets the headlines, the majority of practitioners in the industry go quietly about their business in a professional way, providing important services to satisfied clients. So you need to know there are good ones out there. Follow the guidelines suggested above, and you greatly increase your chances of finding the planner who is right for you.

In the end, if you can match a good financial planner with an equally competent attorney and accountant, you will have assembled a strong advisory team that will provide you with quality support and advice. Such a team will help you achieve your short- and long-term objectives.

11

"Dad Always Liked You Best!"—Part II

*Estate planning makes sense—and dollars, too—for
business owners and their families*

James Keefe sat nervously in my office.

Until the day before, he had been president of Keefe Automotive Sales, one of the Rocky Mountains' largest new car dealerships. Now he was out of a job and felt he was a victim. Naturally, his first thought was to sue those responsible for his misfortune. The targets of his wrath were his younger sister and his mother. They had forced him out of the business.

After his father's death, James had received 49 percent of the stock in the family business. Another 49 percent share went to his sister. The remaining 2 percent—the swing vote—was held by their mother.

James's father had brought him into the business early and taught him well. After the founder's death, James assumed all responsibilities for sales and became the key man in the business. His sister, Susan, handled the bookkeeping and other administrative matters. Her husband managed the service department.

Despite the economic slump that hit the Rocky Mountain region in the eighties, the business persevered under James's stewardship. It had a long-standing tradition of service and good name identity because the elder Keefe had pioneered the new car business in the Denver suburbs.

Because of his dedication to the business, James had not spent much time nurturing family relationships. He was less a devoted son to his mother than was his sister a devoted daughter. As their mother aged, she became increasingly susceptible to the influences of her daughter. Family friction continued. A confrontation was inevitable.

James had always assumed that his superior abilities and position as president and board chairman in the company would enable him to win any family showdown. He was wrong. At a special meeting of the board of directors, James was removed from his posts and given three months' severance pay—after he had worked twenty-five years in the business.

James naturally felt he had been victimized. And he was! But not so much by his sister and mother as by his deceased father. By failing in the most important remaining task in his life—*to plan his estate*—the elder Keefe made his son an unintended victim.

If James's father had asked—and answered—five critical questions, he could have assured the future of his business and his family. Instead, a legal battle that would cost $200,000 and tear the family apart was about to ensue. It would forever end the elder Keefe's dream of a close-knit, happy, family-run business.

The questions the elder Keefe should have addressed are listed below. Your thoughtful answers to these questions, followed by appropriate implementation, may well prevent a similar experience in your own family.

1. How can I provide for an equitable distribution of my estate among my children?
2. How can I use my business to fuel the growth of my estate outside of my business interests?
3. How do I provide for my family's income needs, especially those of my spouse and dependent children, after my death?
4. How can I help preserve my assets from the claims of creditors during my lifetime and at my death?
5. How can I minimize or eliminate estate taxes?

Before analyzing these questions further, let's first review the techniques to avoid giving Uncle Sam more than is necessary.

Estate Taxation

Did you know that estate taxes are voluntary? Unlike income, social security, or excise taxes, estate taxes can be totally avoided. Nevertheless, the government collected more than $8 billion in 1987. How come?

After practicing in the estate planning arena for more than fifteen years, I've concluded that there are only three reasons for this aberration, all based on ignorance: first, ignorance of what estate planning is; second, ignorance of the high rate of estate taxation once it begins and, third, ignorance of the ultimate impact of estate taxation on the owner's estate as he accumulates wealth during his lifetime.

In short, estate taxes exist for those who ignore the fact that they have estates, they will eventually die, and there is a tax based on the size of their estate when they do die. They almost *deserve* to be taxed.

It is important to know what estate taxes are, know the tools available to minimize or avoid them, and employ those tools to transfer your estate (including your business) to the "objects of your bounty" upon your death. But first, let's define what an estate is. An estate, for federal estate tax purposes, is everything you own or control at death, including life insurance proceeds and jointly owned property.

What Is the Estate Tax System?

The federal government imposes an estate tax when two conditions are present: (1) You have departed this earth and (2) your estate is worth at least $600,000. (If your estate is worth less than that, you may stop reading here—the IRS exempts you.)

At the $600,000 level, your estate will be taxed at 37

percent. The rate quickly rises to 45 percent at $1.5 million and tops off at 55 percent at $3 million.

For example, if your estate is $1 million at your death, the estate tax payable is $153,000 ($1 million less $600,000 equals $400,000 times almost 40 percent equals $153,000). On an estate of $1.5 million, the tax is $363,000; on $2.5 million, it's $833,000; and on $5 million, the tax is over $2.2 million.

Obviously the government is a major benefactor of your lifelong efforts to increase the value of your business. There, at the end of the line, stands the IRS with its hands outstretched, palms upward, and all of the enforcement tools and years of experience behind it.

So what chance do you have to avoid or at least minimize your estate taxes? You must take the following critical path.

How to Avoid or Minimize Estate Taxes

First, you must make full use of the $600,000 unified credit amount that you can leave at your death without paying any taxes. If your total estate, for example, is $1.2 million, the potential estate tax is $235,000.

This $600,000 exclusion is also available to your spouse. Through the use of the marital deduction and a "family trust" (also called a credit trust), a total estate of $1.2 million may pass to your children without any estate tax consequences. Let's examine how this is done.

The *marital deduction* is the second primary means to eliminate or reduce estate taxes. This is a total deduction from taxation of all amounts passing from a decedent to his spouse, either as gifts or at death. Even if your estate is $50 billion, if you leave everything to your spouse at your death, there are *no federal estate taxes. Period.*

This sounds great. And it is, at least at the time the first spouse dies. But there's a hidden trap. When the surviving spouse also dies, there is no longer a marital deduction on any property previously passed to her because of the marital deduction. The only deduction that remains is the $600,000 exclusion. In this case the entire estate tax burden then normally falls on the surviving children.

As we've seen, on an estate worth $1.2 million, the total estate tax is $235,000 when the surviving spouse dies. This tax can be completely avoided in estates of $1.2 million or less by making sure that the $600,000 exclusion is used in each estate—both the husband's and the wife's. DeWayne and Connie Smith provide an example.

The Smiths, in their late thirties, had two young children, and all of their assets were held entirely in joint tenancy. Their business was worth $500,000, their home had an equity of $100,000, outside investments and personal property were worth $100,000, and they each had life insurance of $250,000 payable to each other.

As their estate was initially structured, there would be no taxes when the first spouse died since the surviving spouse would receive everything. However, when the surviving spouse died, there would be estate taxes of $235,000.

I explained to the Smiths that the estate tax consequences of not doing any further estate planning was to pay $235,000 of unnecessary taxes. Both insisted, however, that if DeWayne died first Connie should receive the benefit of the entire estate to satisfy her lifetime needs. That was more important to them than saving estate taxes. But then I explained that they could save the taxes *and* accomplish that goal.

First I recommended that the joint tenancy on all of their assets be severed and the assets retitled so that each spouse owned approximately $600,000 of assets in his or her own name. For DeWayne this meant the $250,000 of life insurance would remain his as well as $350,000 worth of business interest. For Connie this meant the $250,000 of life insurance on her life would remain in her name along with the remaining business interest of $150,000, the home, and the personal property.

In the case of the Smiths, after equalizing the estates, we created wills with trust provisions. The effect of the wills was to place the first $600,000 of a spouse's estate in a *family trust* for the benefit of the surviving spouse and children. Accordingly, when the first spouse died (it made no difference who died first, since their estates were equalized—a crucial planning point), the $600,000 owned by the decedent would go into a trust for the survivor. As trustee, the surviving spouse would receive all of the income for the rest of his or her life and have significant control over the use of the money in the trust; yet, for estate tax purposes, only the amount of money owned in their own name would be includable in the estate when the surviving spouse died. This is true because the trust created at the death of the first spouse was designed to place just enough restrictions on the right of access so that the IRS would not consider the amount in that trust to be includable in the surviving spouse's estate as well.

The net result? When the first spouse dies, there will be no estate taxes. Instead, $600,000 will go into a family trust and will be deducted under the $600,000 exclusion. If the decedent spouse had more than $600,000, the rest goes to the surviving spouse via a provision in the will, and this amount qualifies for the marital deduction. So there is never an estate tax when the first spouse dies.

When the surviving spouse dies—assuming the combined estates still total $1.2 million—there is still no estate tax, because the surviving spouse's estate consisted of only $600,000. Although the surviving spouse had the use of the $600,000 left in trust, that amount is not part of the surviving spouse's estate for estate tax purposes.

The net result is an estate tax savings of $235,000.

The trust typically continues for the benefit of the surviving children and, eventually, is terminated. The remaining amounts are then distributed to the children at ages Connie and DeWayne deemed appropriate.

We've seen how estates less than $1.2 million can be transferred to a younger generation without estate taxation. How about larger estates?

The short answer is, If your combined estates exceed $1.2 million and you don't leave the excess to charity, be prepared to pay an estate tax.

Since most people don't want to leave the rest of their estate only to charity, they must during their lifetime reduce the size of their estate if it already exceeds $1.2 million. Or they can minimize its growth.

Of course, it usually makes no sense to either reduce your

estate or avoid growth unless that excess amount passes to your spouse and children.

Reducing the Taxable Estate

As we've seen, the three methods of avoiding estate taxes are (1) making full use of the $600,000 exclusion in both spouses' estates, (2) using the charitable estate tax deduction to avoid taxes on estates valued at more than $1.2 million, and (3) reducing estates that exceed $1.2 million.

The easiest way to do the latter is to give away an asset—especially life insurance. Let's see how this could have worked with DeWayne and Connie Smith.

Instead of the business being worth $500,000, assume its value is $1 million. The total estate then is $1.7 million, including $500,000 in life insurance. Even if we maximize the use of the $600,000 unified credit at each death, about $200,000 in estate taxes will be due when the second spouse dies.

On the other hand, if we were able to remove the life insurance from taxability we could eliminate all estate taxes while allowing the surviving spouse and children to be the beneficiaries of the life insurance.

This is accomplished by transferring ownership of life insurance out of the estate of the older generation (the parents) to an *irrevocable life insurance trust*. This is a document that, once signed by you, can never be changed, altered, or terminated. However, if properly set up it can still be flexible enough to provide benefits among the family members. It operates just like the family trust used by the Smiths. After both parents have died, the proceeds are distributed to the children tax free.

Another aspect of not owning assets at death involves giving property away during your lifetime (see Chapter 8).

For a variety of reasons, not all transfers of business interests are completed during the owner's lifetime. The business may be too valuable, making the gift taxes too expensive; the surviving spouse may want to remain active in the business and in control of it for as long as he or she wishes; the owner may have been unwilling to relinquish control of the business until his or her death; or the owner may have been in the process of giving or selling the business to the children.

Whatever the reason, most businesses don't seem to be transferred to a younger generation until the death of the older generation. That's why it's important to have a planned disposition of your business interest. The planning can be expressed in a will or trust, or in a buy-and-sell agreement with offspring who will remain active in the business.

Without doubt, the preferred method of transferring a business interest is by a binding buy-and-sell agreement where the death buyout is funded in whole or in part with life insurance on the owner's life. With this agreement in place, several assurances are made.

The children who will remain in the business and control it know that at your death they will become the controlling owners of the business. The agreements obligate your estate to do that. Conversely, you are assured that upon your death cash will be received by the estate in exchange for stock that may otherwise have little value in the hands of a spouse who has never been active in the business.

In short, the buy-and-sell agreement is a covenant between you and the children who will succeed you in business. It is a promise that protects you and the children, and a great benefit to those heirs for whom money is more important than owning stock in your business.

Historically, a buy-and-sell agreement has also been used to help establish value for the stock when it transfers at the owner's death. The agreement still remains valuable for this purpose, but you need to keep in mind that the IRS will view with suspicion a transfer between a parent and a child as being other than arms length and may therefore subject the stock value to its standard valuation tests (see Chapter 7).

In the absence of a buy-and-sell agreement, stock can be transferred by your will or trust documents. If you do not specifically make a bequest of the stock to your children, it will pass as part of the "residue" of your estate, and each residuary heir will be entitled to an equal portion of the stock—the worst possible distribution of the company's ownership. At the very least, a specific bequest should be made in your will directing the stock to the appropriate person or persons.

In many situations it's simply not appropriate to do this. You may not want the business continued by the family after your death, family members may be too young or inexperienced to assume control, or they may not want to be involved in the business after your death. The primary method of dealing with any of these situations is to place the ownership in trust. You tell the trustee what to do through the powers and restrictions given him in the trust document.

In a sense you can continue to rule the business from the grave. For example, you could require the trust to continue to own the business interest until younger children attain maturity, at which time they can be given the option to take over the family business or let it be sold. The trustee could be instructed to hire or appoint a key employee or group of employees to run the business until a specified date. The trustee can be given the power to sell the business when certain events related to the business occur. A trust can be designed so that the trustees are given only the power to elect a board of directors consisting of a group or category of individuals you describe in the trust instrument.

In short, trusts are flexible and can be designed to account for the specific conditions and circumstances of your business. They normally are not permanent solutions, but can provide for proper management and control until it's time to transfer, sell, or liquidate the stock.

Now let's return to those key questions we raised early in this chapter.

How Can I Provide for an Equitable Distribution of My Estate Among My Children?

Parents normally want to give equal amounts of their estate to their surviving children, regardless of how active each child was in the business. The problem with having this provision in a will is that each child will get not only an equal amount of the business, but also an equal amount of the *nonbusiness assets.*

This ignores the fact the owner may have already given large portions of the business to the business-active child; it also ignores the fundamental objective of getting the entire business interest to those children active in the business while giving the rest of the children a disproportionate share in the balance of the estate.

The problem of providing for *fair* (notice I did not say *equal*) distribution to all of the children is illustrated by the Aurora Scaffolding Corporation. This case reflects most of the problems—and opportunities—involved in the estate planning process.

My company had represented Aurora Scaffolding for many years. Aurora rented and installed scaffolding systems on commercial sites. Like all construction-related firms, its economic fortunes rose and fell with unnerving regularity. However, its founder, Mike Fletcher, was a survivor—not only of the ups and downs of his business but of a disabling injury at the age of 51. That experience made him a true believer in the estate planning process. Consequently I found him in my office shortly after his release from one of our local hospitals.

Mike arrived with a list of objectives he had carefully prepared. He wanted to begin an immediate transition of management—and ultimately control—to his youngest son, Patrick, who had been working in the business almost five years. Mike was motivated not simply out of a desire to benefit Patrick, but more importantly to provide a mechanism for getting money out of the business for Mike's own benefit should he become fully disabled.

There were no other likely candidates to buy his stock, so the fact that Patrick wanted to eventually own the business enabled Mike to make that decision earlier than he had planned.

Mike's other primary assets were the building where his company conducted its business and which he owned personally, his residence, outside savings of about $250,000, and life insurance of almost $400,000.

Because Mike had neglected to obtain adequate disability income insurance, his second objective was to ensure that he would have adequate monies available to him in the event of his disability.

Mike described his other objectives:

- He wanted to provide a comfortable life-style for his wife, Sharon, in the event of his death.
- Primarily at her insistance, he wanted to provide for an equitable distribution of the estate to his other son after both he and his wife died.
- Finally, he was reluctant to pay any estate taxes.

These concerns are typical. Retirement income. Disability income. Family income for surviving family members. Fair distribution of the family's estate among children. Avoidance of estate taxes. Aren't they your concerns also?

We addressed all of Mike's concerns by first observing the procedures discussed in Chapter 10. Again, these procedures are to:

1. Establish your objectives.
2. Establish a timetable.
3. Determine ownership structure.
4. Obtain a consensus for your plan.
5. Implement the plan.

You may want to review the Cribari family example in Chapter 10. The situation is similar to the Fletcher family example.

How did we approach these questions? First we quantified Mike's objectives. Mike and his wife lived comfortably, but not lavishly, on his salary of $90,000 a year. He wanted to continue this amount as long as he lived. At Mike's death his wife could live comfortably on $60,000 per year. We reviewed Mike's estate.

His simplified balance sheet looked like this:

Fair market value of business	$400,000
Net equity in building	100,000

Net equity in residence	$125,000
Outside liquid investments	50,000
Profit sharing plan	250,000
Life insurance	400,000

Mike's total estate, for estate tax purposes, was $1,325,000. The portion that could produce income for him and his family was $700,000, derived from a profit-sharing plan of $250,000, outside savings of $50,000, and business interests of $400,000.

The building would eventually become an income-producing investment. However, Mike had elected to have a fifteen-year amortization on his loan when he purchased the building eight years earlier. This resulted in high monthly payments, so there would be no significant net cash flow for another seven years, at which time another $3,000 per month would be available for income needs. Of course, in the event of Mike's disability or death, his salary would stop. So, while the business was still worth $400,000, it would produce no income to Mike. Liquidating the business would probably yield about $200,000.

The plan we finally devised looked primarily to the business to provide Mike with income needs. The accountants determined that the fair market value of the business was $400,000 and estimated it would likely increase steadily in future years.

Mike decided to give Patrick 49 percent of the business, worth $200,000, in order to remove half of the future appreciation of the business from Mike's estate. He also entered into a deferred compensation agreement with the company. The agreement provided for a $50,000 annual payment to Mike if he terminated employment for any reason other than his death. In that case, his estate would receive nothing under the deferred compensation agreement. The agreement was originally designed to run ten years.

Mike then entered into a buy-and-sell agreement with Patrick so that he and the business became obligated to purchase Mike's stock if he left the company for any reason, including death or disability. The purchase price was the fair market value of Mike's remaining stock, worth $200,000 at present.

Now we redesigned the Fletcher family estate plan. We prepared an *irrevocable life insurance trust* and transferred all of the life insurance into it. The beneficiaries were Mike's wife, Sharon, and both children. The oldest son, William, would receive the first $200,000 of the remaining trust estate at his mother's death. Thereafter, the two sons would divide equally whatever amount was left, if any.

The $200,000 additional benefit to William is an attempt to equalize the $200,000 lifetime gift to Patrick. I say "attempt" because if their mother lives for another thirty-five years (her probable life expectancy), William would not receive any money until then, while Patrick has enjoyed the $200,000 gift for those thirty-five years.

On the other hand, when William does receive his share of the inheritance, it will likely be in cash or its equivalent, while Patrick receives his share in the form of closely held stock. This will bind Patrick to the family business, including all the risks attendant in owning a small business. His presence will provide the continuity of management required during a buyout of his father's stock as well as the deferred compensation.

Because Patrick is taking more risk, it can be argued that he is earning the stock being given to him since he has agreed to stay on and provide a means for his father to receive money for his retirement or death—either through the stock sale or the deferred compensation payments.

In looking at equalizing an estate, the business owner is usually faced with the fact that it is desirable to give stock to the child active in the business during the owner's lifetime and to give other assets to the nonactive child or children only after the death of the surviving spouse. This results in a substantial timing difference. However, the child active in the business will find his share of the family estate at risk. It is difficult to quantify these factors. What is critical here is not giving an exact amount, but giving what family members believe to be fair.

In an ideal situation, the nonactive child, William, would be given assets along with his business-active brother during their mother's lifetime. In most circumstances, however, this is impractical; the business owner will need all of the income-producing assets available for him and his spouse.

We also prepared a buy-and-sell agreement that provided for the purchase by Patrick or the corporation of Mike's stock in the event of his death, disability, or retirement. Typically, in a buy-and-sell agreement, we would recommend that the property used in the business—in this case, the building and construction yard—be purchased by the business-active child, along with the business interest. In this situation, however, the building will become an income-producing asset for the elder Fletcher and his wife as soon as the mortgage is paid off. Therefore, the decision was made to retain the building to assure rental income for Mike and Sharon starting seven years later.

The balance of the estate plan was designed to be fairly standard. It created marital trusts and family trusts in Mike's estate plan, thereby protecting an additional $400,000 from estate taxation at Mike's death.

Note that since Mike gifted $200,000 during his lifetime, he used up $200,000 of the unified credit. This allowed only $400,000 to be placed in the family trust at his death, instead of the normal $600,000. His wife still has her $600,000 amount available to her at her death.

Because the life insurance trust will avoid estate taxes on the life insurance and we have protected $400,000 at Mike's death, estate taxes are totally avoided. Without such planning, the total estate tax amount at Sharon's death would have been approximately $300,000.

The deferred compensation plan was designed to begin payment either when Mike became disabled or retired. To design the plan, we analyzed the likely cash flow abilities of the company. If Mike were to become disabled, his stock would first be repurchased by the corporation. But the company would be unable to pay for both the repurchase and the deferred compensation. Therefore, we decided to delay any deferred compensation payment until the buyout of the stock was completed.

The amount needed from the corporation to sustain Mike's $90,000 per year life-style—the net return of available assets—was approximately $75,000 per year. With Mike's business interest valued at $200,000, this meant that the business would need to pay out $75,000 a year for three years to purchase Mike's stock. Accordingly, the deferred compensation agreement was designed to begin three years after Mike terminated employment due to disability. The compensation would then begin, paying $75,000 per year for four years, after which it would decrease to $25,000 per year for fifteen years. By then, however, the Fletchers would begin getting $4,000 in rental income from the building.

As designed, the plan assured that a stream of income would flow from the business directly to the Fletchers for the rest of Mike's life. At Mike's death Patrick would be responsible for the purchase of his father's stock, but the company would not be under any obligation to pay deferred compensation. That is true because his mother's needs would be less than hers and Mike's combined, and her needs could be satisfied from the income of the irrevocable life insurance trust and the income from other investments and the building rentals.

We've seen from the Mike Fletcher/Aurora Scaffolding example how difficult it can be to distribute the business owner's estate equitably between children while providing for the surviving spouse. In allocating the business interest to the business-active child or children during the owner's lifetime, the hardest aspect is to weigh the value of the gift now against the future bequest to the nonactive child or children.

The following factors need to be analyzed:

- Is the business-active child, in effect, paying for the business now through lowered compensation, more working hours, and greater risk?
- Is the business-active child adding to the business's value through his or her efforts? If so, he should not have to pay for that effort by receiving a reduced share of the ultimate estate.
- Has the active child, by continuing in the business after your retirement, become a critical element in your retirement plan by ensuring that the corporation can pay any deferred compensation or stock purchase fund? If so, the means by which you tie him or her into the business—the golden handcuffs—may be the gifting of stock.

We saw how that happened to Patrick Fletcher. If you are the offspring-owner of 49 percent of the stock of a company, you are likely to work longer, harder, and with an ultimate objective of making sure your father leaves the business under terms he has established.

Hopefully, the transfer of the business interest to the business-active child is only one element in the owner's estate planning. A buy-and-sell agreement is fundamental. The life-time income needs of the owner and his dependents must be factored in. This requires coordination between the use of traditional estate planning concepts, such as an irrevocable life insurance trust, with the gift of the business interest to create parity among the children.

Why Should I Use My Business to Fuel the Growth of My Estate Outside My Business Interest?

The *techniques* for using your business to fuel the growth of your estate outside the business were described in Chapter 10, but the *reasons* you need to encourage the growth of your estate outside of your business are compelling and worth reviewing.

If you are like most owners, your assets are much like the Fletcher family's. Primarily, your assets consist of your business, a personal residence, a few personal assets, and little else. This has several consequences.

1. Your ownership interest in the business is probably illiquid and therefore, like Mike Fletcher, it will be difficult to get much for your business interest when you retire without advanced planning.
2. If the bulk of your estate is in the business, it's subject to the claims of business as well as nonbusiness creditors and, of course, to the ongoing risks of any business.
3. By increasing the value of your nonbusiness estate, assets become available that can ultimately be given to children who are not active in the business.
4. Transferring wealth from the business to you is a natural part of preparing for retirement or any other type of ownership transfer.

And finally, income generated from assets outside of the business will normally not be subject to earned income taxes, such as FICA, and it provides a base for family income.

Mike Fletcher used two primary vehicles to move income from the business to himself—his retirement plan and the purchase of a building outside of the corporation. Without that advance preparation he could not be assured of adequate income in the event of his disability, retirement, or death.

Planning makes the difference between living comfortably and living precariously. You have worked too hard not to enjoy the fruits of your labor. Start by planning now.

How Do I Provide for My Family's Income Needs After My Death?

In addition to planning for your family's income during your lifetime, your spouse and dependent children will have needs after your death. There are several components that address these needs.

One component will be the nonbusiness income-producing assets that you created during your lifetime. Another will be getting the business value to your family by means of a buy-and-sell agreement that, at your death, requires the active children, a co-owner, or a third party to purchase your business interest in exchange for money, ideally funded by life insurance.

The third component is to design your estate plan so that the assets benefit your spouse while ultimately passing to your children with the fewest tax consequences. This is best achieved by creating trusts to take advantage of the unified credit ($600,000 amount) and marital deductions as well as use of an irrevocable life insurance trust funded with life insurance that is paid for primarily by the business under a split dollar plan.

Split dollar agreements are discussed in Chapter 9. Basically they require the business to pay the bulk of the premiums while the death proceeds are owned and payable by the life insurance trust. At the death of the insured, the corporation gets back the cash value to compensate it for making the premium payments, while the balance of the death proceeds are paid to the life insurance trust without estate tax consequences. This is a way of having the business and, indirectly, the active children in the business pay for life insurance premiums benefiting the spouse and, perhaps, the other children.

How Can I Help Preserve My Assets From the Claims of Creditors During My Lifetime and at My Death?

The second most frequently asked question I get ("How much will this cost?" is first) is "Can I transfer my assets to my wife and avoid my creditors?"

My response is "It depends. To get the exact answer, it will cost you. . . ."

Just kidding. Most owners are deeply concerned about the litigation crisis in our society. They are anxious about spending a lifetime building up assets only to have one lawsuit take away everything. For that reason they want to transfer assets from their name to another—usually their spouse, or sometimes a trust for their children. Then, if they are sued, they will be "judgment proof"—that is, there will be no assets to collect from in their name.

The difficulty with this approach is that creditors, not debtors, make the laws in this country. There is a law in many states known as the Fraudulent Conveyance Act. It provides that if a person transfers property to another with the intent to delay, hinder, or defraud a current or future creditor, then that transfer is void and the asset so transferred is attachable as part of the debtor's estate.

If the transfer is to a close family member, the general rule is that there is a presumption that the conveyance was fraudulent. That means that you—the transferor—have the burden of proving that the transfer to your spouse or children was not fraudulent. If litigation had already been threatened or started, any transfer to a family member for less than fair and adequate consideration is suspicious; it is likely to be attacked as fraudulent.

If a transfer to a family member is to be made, then it must be made well *before* litigation is even threatened. And there must be a reason that can be established—other than to avoid creditors. If you can demonstrate that the transfer is part of your estate planning and income tax planning, then you may have established an acceptable reason.

Estate planning goals are often accomplished by equalizing estates between husbands and wives. Since the husband, who is usually the owner of the business, normally has the bulk of the estate, it makes sense to transfer at least $600,000 worth of assets to the wife.

Finally, another reason to transfer assets is to fund a children's trust for college education purposes. These trusts may be funded with as much as $50,000 to $100,000 of assets per child.

Summary

Estate planning is a process that continues throughout your lifetime. The degree of involvement—or neglect—you pay to this process will be felt by your loved ones long after you are gone. Thorough estate planning should accomplish these goals:

1. To provide for family income needs, especially those of your spouse and dependent children, after your death.
2. To minimize or eliminate estate taxes.

3. To provide for a fair, but not necessarily equal, distribution of your estate among your children, both during your lifetime and at death.

4. To preserve your assets from the claims of creditors during your lifetime and at death.

12

Ten Steps to Success

Summarizing the actions you must take now to achieve your owner-based objectives

I've packed a lot of information into this book, mindful that sometimes too much information can be discouraging and overwhelming. Therefore, you may be happy to learn that I have no additional facts to burden you with. Instead, I simply want to conclude by showing you how to integrate the principles you've learned into your daily business practice.

First, let's review the basic premise of this book:

At some point, every owner leaves his or her business—voluntarily or otherwise. At that time the owner will want to receive the maximum amount of money in order to accomplish personal financial income and estate planning goals.

To that end, I've shown you first how to create and preserve wealth for your business interest by looking at the business from an ownership standpoint rather than a management or employee standpoint. Then, in the second part, I recognize that eventually you will transfer your ownership interest—most likely the most significant asset you'll ever own. That's why it's necessary to plan for that certainty so that you can exercise maximum control over that outcome. Finally, the last part of this book deals with your relationship to the business as an individual and shows you how to best use the business to accumulate wealth for your personal use, decrease your tax burden, and create a valuable estate for your heirs.

How to Begin Planning

Although I'm pleased that you've come this far in the book, I now encourage you to go even farther—to apply your newly acquired knowledge, to put it to work for you. Do this and you will be starting down the path toward attaining your owner-based objectives.

Listed below are ten essential steps to start you down that path. In essence, these steps summarize what you have been reading, so that if you take these actions now you will be applying what you have learned.

Step One

Acknowledge to yourself that sooner or later you will leave your business. With that in mind, resolve to pursue these three owner-based objectives:

1. To create and preserve value in your business.
2. To provide a way to exchange that value for money.
3. To use your business to attain your personal financial and estate planning goals.

Step Two

Form an advisory team consisting of an accountant, a lawyer, and a financial planner. Tap this resource while conducting your fiscal year-end meeting. Ask for a legal audit. Become familiar with the potential litigation traps that lay hidden in your business.

Step Three

Introduce methods and programs to motivate and keep your key employee(s). This will help create and preserve value in your business as well as build a potential market when you decide to sell.

Step Four

Don't try to become a tax expert, but familiarize yourself with the fundamentals of the tax laws. Use your advisors to keep your tax burden from impeding your value-building strategies, especially with regard to your retirement plans.

Step Five

Set a retirement date, even if it's only tentative. Determine how much money you will need when you retire. As time passes, work with your advisory team, especially your financial planner, to fine-tune and adjust this goal.

Step Six

Determine the value of your business using only valid methods accepted by the IRS.

Step Seven

Examine each of the four ways you can leave your business. Determine which way would be best for you. If you want to transfer ownership to your child, use the six-step planning process to achieve clear communication and avoid a family dispute.

Step Eight

Ask your advisory team to draw up the most important document in your business—the business continuity agreement.

Step Nine

Ask your advisory team to initiate the five-step process to prepare a comprehensive financial plan that will help you achieve your personal financial goals.

Step Ten

Ask your advisory team to design an estate plan that meets your personal objectives. Be certain your money will go where you want it to when you die—and that Uncle Sam gets no more of it than his fair share.

To help with your planning, take a minute now to review the fiscal year-end outline shown in Exhibit 12-1.

Under each heading I've inserted the chapter(s) in this book that pertain to that point in parentheses. Thus, as you proceed with your planning, the process itself will continually reintroduce the points raised in this book, reminding you to consider them as you build your plan.

At times one issue may predominate; it might be income taxes considerations or concerns about business continuity. Rather than dealing with these as stand-alone issues, the planning process will allow you to integrate them with all the other elements in your planning. Furthermore, by using the fiscal year-end review to work on your planning, you automatically receive the benefits that result from working with your advisory team.

A Final Word About Your Advisors

Throughout this book I've constantly referred to your use of an advisory team consisting of an attorney, an accountant, and a financial planner. Their work may also be supplemented by a business consultant. These professionals cannot increase your sales or lower the production costs of your product or help you locate or become a good manager. But they represent the only resource available to help you attain the ultimate

Exhibit 12-1. Fiscal year-end planning outline.

I. Review of Business Income Tax Status.

    A. Initial determination of income tax liability. (4)*

    B. Existing methods of reducing income tax liability. (4)

    C. Consideration of new methods to reduce income tax liability as appropriate. (4)

II. Additional Corporate Considerations.

    A. Business continuity. (6,9)

    B. Business expansion/contraction. (3,4,6,9)

    C. Employee considerations. (3)

    D. Banking contracts and forms. (2)

    E. Banking considerations. (2)

    F. Miscellaneous. (1,2,3,4,5)

III. Individual Planning Considerations.

    A. Current income tax status and methods to reduce income tax liability. (4)

    B. Financial planning considerations. (10)

    C. Estate planning considerations. (5,8,11,12)

IV. Goal-Setting Conclusions.

    A. Business goals. (1,2,6,12)

    B. Individual goals. (1,6,8,12,13)

V. Business Opportunities (1,2)

---

*Chapter where subject is discussed.

business objectives I've described. Armed with an expertise based on training, education, and years of experience in dealing with other business owners, they will help keep you focused on these objectives.

The team members must be compatible, so that they can work together to help you achieve the final victory of transferring your valuable business interest in exchange for money to accomplish your personal goals. They must also be judicious in introducing planning issues at appropriate times. Certainly, it is not necessary to resolve every issue I've raised at the first planning meeting; but over a period of years all of those issues should be addressed, resolved and, if necessary, reconsidered time and again.

In short, to the extent the issues I've identified become overwhelming, your team of advisors must act as counselors and perhaps teachers so that you can see the whole picture, yet focus only on those issues that are timely.

Many professionals have all the skills necessary to help you. Yet they haven't organized those skills in the fashion described here, nor have they worked with other professionals as a team. Because all facets of business, including planning, are becoming increasingly complex, you can no longer allow your individual advisors to work independently of each other. They must provide each other with advice and input to enhance their value to you.

Take the time now to assess your advisors' qualifications as well as their willingness and capacity to work in a planning mode with you and other team members. If in the past they haven't helped you with the issues I've raised, ask them to read this book. In the end, if they don't pass muster, it's time to find new team members.

In sum, keep your ownership objectives continually in mind; commit yourself to the planning process; and find and use professionals whose training, experience, and disposition lend themselves to making your ultimate objectives become a reality. Do these things and you will greatly increase your chances to establish a successful business, achieve satisfaction, and eventually leave your business under circumstances that are most favorable to you.

Good luck.

Index

227